THE VANI

Book 1 – The Migration to the Rhine

by
Edmund Karlsson

List of Characters (those characters believed to be actual historical figures appear in bold. Note that all dates are C.E. [A.D.] unless otherwise stated.)

The companions of Gaeseric.

Gaeseric, king of the Vandals and Alans, 427 to 473. Son of Godigsel and Flavia. Also known as Gaeser, a shortened form of his name, and as Gisselitta when young.

Marcus Flavius Eutychianus, the narrator and half-brother of Gaeseric. Known to the Vandals as Scuta and, in later life, as Master Marcus, to his school pupils and tutors.

Axxa, companion and senior Vandal guard.

Coccas, Trevingi Goth and companion of Gaeser. Twin brother of Traso.

Fredobodus, also known as Fredo, Quadi and companion of Gaeser.

Ingamar, Alemanni and companion of Gaeser.

Kitan, companion and Vandal guard.

Otte, companion and Vandal guard.

Scarila, Siling Vandal and companion of Gaeser.

Skara, companion and Vandal guard.

Trasovado, also known as Traso, Trevingi Goth and companion of Gaeser. Twin brother of Coccas.

Tzason, son of Asphax, Alan and companion of Gaeser.

Ulli, companion and Vandal guard.

Wada, companion, and Vandal guard.

The friends and family of the companions.

Asphax, Tzason's father and leader of the Sava valley Alans.

Dagila, granddaughter of Sigibali, brother of Scarila and girlfriend of Gaeser.

Diomedes, Greek *grammaticus*, teacher at the summer palace.

Gibamundus, one of two Vandal co-kings before the migration. Father of Godigsel and grandfather of Gaeser.

Gaius Flavius Eutychianus, *Pretorian Prefect* for Illyricum in 396 and later a consul in Constantinople. Uncle of Scuta.

Godigsel, King of the Vandals from 401 to 406. Father of Gunderic and Gaeser.

Gregor, Greek tutor, and servant to Flavia and, later, Scuta and Gaeser.

Flamma, Gaeser's horse.

Flavia, mother of both Scuta and Gaeser.

Hildiger, Ingamar's father, Alemmani commander of the Pannonian *classis* based at Taurunum.

Hunneric, King of the Vandals and Alans from 477 to 484. Son of Gaeseric.

Indulf, son of Athaulf of the Trevingi Goths.

Kossus, son of Tzason.

Manius, freedman, assistant to Master Marcus and senior tutor at the school.

Marcus Flavius Eutychianus, *Pretorian Prefect* for Illyricum from 388 to 389. Father to Scuta who also had the same Roman *trinoma* - Marcus Flavius Eutychianus.

Safrax, Tzason's Alan bodyguard and later his stepfather.

Shirkar, Tzason's Alano dog.

Vangio, father of Fredo and Quadi commander of the garrison at Sirmium.

Yannas, freedman, assistant to Master Marcus and junior tutor at the school.

Wolf, Gaeser's Alano dog.

Zanthi, a Carthaginian ship captain.

The Romans, (many with barbarian roots)

Aetius, son of a Goth, a Roman hostage of the Goths and then later a hostage of the Huns. De facto ruler of the Western Roman Empire from 433 to 454.

Ambrose, Gallo-Roman and bishop of Mediolanum [Milan].

Arbogast, a Frank, *magister militum* and military strongman behind the usurper Eugenius.

Arcadius, Emperor of the Eastern Roman Empire from 383 to 408. Son of Theodosius. Brother of Honorius.

Ardabur, an Alan, *magister militum* of the Eastern Roman Empire in the 420s. Father of Asper.

Asper, an Alan, son of Ardabur, *magister militum* and *de facto* ruler of the Eastern Roman Empire during the 450s and 460s.

Basiliscus, Eastern Roman Emperor from 475 to 476.

Constantine III, acclaimed as Emperor by the Roman legions of Britannia in 407, ruled Britannia, Gaul, and Hispania briefly, as a usurper before becoming co-Emperor with Honorius from 409 to 411.

Eugenious, usurper against Theodosius for the Western Roman Empire.

Gratian, Emperor of the Western Roman Empire from 367 to 383.

Hadrian, Emperor of the Roman Empire from 117 to 138.

Honorius, Emperor of the Western Roman Empire from 383 to 423. Son of Theodosius. Brother of Arcadius.

Marcian, Emperor of the Eastern Roman Empire from 450 to 457. Raised to the purple by Asper. Previously Asper's personal assistant.

Marcus Aurelias, Emperor of the Roman Empire from 270 to 275.

Studios, urban prefect in Constantinople in 404.

Serena, the adopted daughter of Theodosius and wife of Stilico. She lived at the court of Honorius, her stepbrother.

Stilico, son of a Vandal cavalry officer, *de facto* ruler of the Western Roman Empire from 395 to 408.

Theodosius, Emperor of the Roman Empire from 379 to 395. The last man to rule the combined Empire.

Valentinian I, Emperor of the Western Roman Empire from 364 to 375.

Valentinian III, Emperor of the Western Roman Empire from 425 to 455, grandson of Theodosius.

The Barbarians

Abtin, leader of the Roxolani warriors forming part of the Alan forces, a key element of the Roman army of Italy, at the battle of Polentia.

Alaric, king of the Trevingi Goths part of the merged Goth group later termed the Visigoths.

Athaulf, king of the Visigoths from 411 to 415. Father of Indulf.

Attila, co-king of the Huns from 434 to 445 with his brother Bleda. Sole king from 445 to 453.

Beremut, Siling Vandal amber trader.

Bleda, Attila's brother and co-king of the Huns from 434 to 445.

Childeric, king of the Salian Franks from 458 to 481.

Crixos, leader of the Lacringi Vandals.

Fredbal, war king of the Siling Vandals during the migration.

Fritigern, leader of the Trevingi Goths at the battle of Adrianople and during the subsequent Goth wars.

Goar, leader of the Alan band that migrated from the Tisza valley to eventually settle in Brittany.

Guntha, a Vandal *ala* commander.

Heremigarius, Suebe, brother of Hermeric.

Hermeric, King of the Suebes from 406 to 438.

Holz, Siling Vandal and forest guide.

Marobus, sub-king of the southern Quadi tribes during the invasion of Raetia in 401.

Mundzak, a Hun, son of Uldin and father of Attila and Bleda.

Obadus, briefly war king of the Asding Vandals before Godigsel.

Octar, son of Uldin, co-king of the Huns from 413 to 430 with his brother Rugila.

Odovacer, king of Italy from 476 to 493. He was either a Sciri or a Goth.

Radagarius, leader of the mainly Goth invasion of Italy in 406.

Respendial, king of the northern Tisza valley Alans during the migration.

Rugila, son of Uldin, co-king of the Huns from 413 to 430 with his brother Octar. Sole king from 430 to 435.

Sangiban, leader of Goar's Alans at the battle of the Catalaunian Fields in 451.

Saurus, Gruethungi Goth who became a leading commander in the Western Roman army.

Saul, Alan who was commanding general of the Roman forces at the battle of Polentia.

Scorpius, successful chariot race driver at the Sirmium hippodrome.

Sigibali, co-king of the Siling Vandals before the migration. Grandfather of Dagila and Scarila.

Sigirus, brother of Saurus, briefly king of the Visigoths in 415.

Uldin, leader of the Huns north of the Danube, later the first established King of the Huns from 400 to 412. Father of Octar, Rugila and Mundzak.

Ulfred, Vandal trooper and military chaplain.

Vannius, sub-king of the northern Quadi tribes before the migration.

Velda, leader of the Hun forces in the Western Roman army during the invasion of Radagarius.

Wolfila, Goth of Greek descent who is credited with translating the Bible into Gothic.

Other historical figures mentioned.

Alexander the Great, otherwise Alexander III of Macedon. Ruled the Macedonian Empire from 336 to 323 BCE. Conquered the known world by the age of thirty creating an Empire stretching from Greece to India. Believed to be undefeated in battle and, on that basis, one of history's greatest ever generals. Alexander's companions were the elite cavalry of his army within which his chosen companions were his boyhood friends who acted as Alexander's elite bodyguards.

Arrian, Roman military commander during the reign of Hadrian who fought against the Alans and subsequently wrote '*Contra Alanos*,' or 'The order of battle against the Alans,' amongst many other works.

Cicero, a Roman senator, orator, lawyer, philosopher, and writer who lived during the last days of the Roman Republic.

Hannibal, a Carthaginian general who commanded the forces of Carthage in the second Punic War against Rome. Hannibal invaded Italy by crossing the Alps with North African war elephants. He won a succession of victories against the Romans at Trebia, Lake Trasimene and Cannae. The heavy losses he inflicted on the Romans left Rome defenceless, but Hannibal chose not to take the city. Regarded as one of the greatest military commanders in history, he lived from 247 to 181 BCE.

Herodotus was an Ancient Greek writer and historian who lived from 484 to 425 BCE. Considered the father of history and described as such by Cicero. He is sometimes criticized for fanciful elements in his histories including descriptions of the Amazons, female warriors. Archaeological discoveries on the Eurasian steppes suggest that the Scythian and Samartian peoples may indeed have had some tradition of female fighters.

Tiro, Cicero's assistant and servant, who is believed to have recorded Cicero's work using a form of shorthand.

Migration to the Rhine of the Vandals, Alans and Suebes in 406 AD

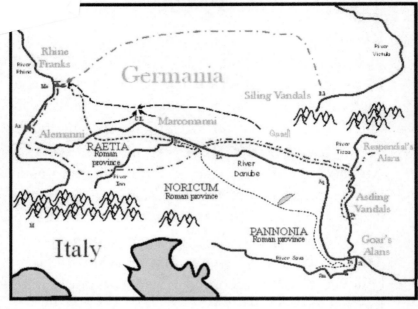

Main migration routes

←----- **Asding Vandals**   ←·− Siling Vandals   ←··− Alans   ←-- Suebes

Summer palace convoy route   --------------

Cities & towns [with modern equivalents]

Ar - Argetorate [Strasbourg],
Aq - Aquincum [Budapest],
Bo - Boiodurum [Passau],
CR - Castra Regina, [Regensburg],
La - Lauriacum [Enns],
M - Mediolanum [Milan],

Mo - Mogontiacum [Mainz],
Pa - Partiscum [Szeged],
Rk - Rakow [Kracow],
Si - Singidunum [Belgrade],
Sm - Sirmium [Stremska],
Tu - Taurunum, [Belgrade]

Place Names and their modern equivalents
(other than those listed above).
Adrianople - Edirne, Turkey.
Amorica - Brittany, France.
Aquileia - a small town close to Venice, Italy.
Augusta Treverom - Trier, Germany.
Augusta Vindelicorum - Augsburg, Germany.
Batavia - Passau, Germany.
Borbetomagus - Worms, Germany.
Bulla Regis - Jendouba, Tunisia.
Carthage - the ruins of Carthage are close to
Tunis, Tunisia.
Castellum Mattiacorum - Mainz-Kastel,
Germany.
Colonia - Cologne, Germany.
Colonia Aelia Mursa - Osijek, Hungary.
Constantinople - Istanbul, Turkey.
Euxine Sea - Black Sea.
Florentia - Florence, Italy.
Germania Inferior (Germania Secunda by the
fourth century) -
            Roman province comprising all the
            territory west of the Rhine including
            modern-day Luxembourg, the
            southern Netherlands, part of Belgium, and
            part of North Rhine-

Westphalia in Germany. The provincial
capital was Cologne.

Germania Superior -

Roman province in modern day Southwest
Germany and the Alsace and Jura regions
of France. The provincial capital was
Mainz.

Gernsheim - a small town on the Rhine near
Darmstadt, Germany.

Lacus Brigantius - Lake Constance on the border
of Switzerland and Germany.

Lacus Pelso - Lake Belaton, Hungary.

Lentia - Linz, Austria.

Lilybaeum - Marsala, Sicily.

Mare Germanicum - North Sea.

Municipium Sopianae - Pecs, Hungary.

Noviomagus - Speyer, Germany.

Noricum -

Roman province in modern day Austria and
parts of Slovenia. The provincial capital
was Virinum in the modern area of
Zollfeld, Austria.

Ovilava - Wels, Austria.

Pannonia -

Roman province in modern day western
Hungary, eastern Austria, northern Croatia
and north-western Serbia. The provincial

capital was Sirmium near modern day Belgrade.

Patavium - Padua, Italy.

Polentia - Pollenzo, Italy.

Raetia -
Roman province in modern day northern Switzerland and southern Germany. The provincial capital was Augsburg.

Vindobona - Vienna, Austria.

Vimincium - Kostolac, Serbia.

List of contents

Prologue - Carthage in year 38 of the Vandal calendar, 477 CE

Chapter 1 - My early childhood

Chapter 2 - My education

Chapter 3 - Alaric and the Trevingi Goths

Chapter 4 - Alaric's grand plan

Chapter 5 - Godigsel's plan

Chapter 6 - The Alemanni marines and the Danube fleet

Chapter 7 - The Vandal and Alan homelands

Chapter 8 - My first battle

Chapter 9 - The aftermath of the battle

Chapter 10 - The Raetian campaign of 401

Chapter 11 - The confrontation with the Roman field army

Chapter 12 - The return to Pannonia

Chapter 13 - A significant day at the hippodrome

Chapter 14 - A visit to a horse farm

Chapter 15 - An emergency visit to the Tisza Valley

Chapter 16 - The Siling Vandals

Chapter 17 - The Marcomanni and the Suebic Federation

Chapter 18 - The invasion of Radagarius of 406

Chapter 19 - The beginnings of the Hun empire

Chapter 20 - The convoy to Raetia and the defeat of Radagarius

Chapter 21 - The return of the Goths

Chapter 22 - Confrontations with the Rhine Franks

Chapter 23 - Before the Battle of Mogontiacum

Chapter 24 - The Battle of Mogontiacum

Chapter 25 - After the Battle of Mogontiacum

Chapter 26 - Crossing the Rhine

"Now the Vandals and the Alani, as we have said before, had been dwelling in both Pannonias by permission of the Roman Emperors. Yet fearing they would not be safe even here if the Goths should return, they crossed over into Gaul."

Jordanes, *Gettica*, 31.161.(written in 550 CE in reference to the crossing of the Rhine by the Vandals, Alans and Suebes in 406 CE).

Prologue

Carthage in year 38 of the Vandal calendar (477 CE)

We walked slowly down from the *Byrsa* hill away from the funeral. I could no longer maintain a faster walk. It was no wonder as I was older than the deceased had been, and he lived well into his eighties. I needed my assistants, Manius and Yannas, on either side of me in case I stumbled on the uneven pathway. Several youths of various ages followed our progress impatiently. Our journey home was short, simply following the *Decumanus Maximus*, the main street of Carthage, towards the harbour. Looking out towards the sea we could see the hive of activity that was the commercial harbour. Hundreds of trading ships were tied up to over fifty moles jutting into the sea for more than a mile from the Antonine Baths on the left down to the *Mandrikon*, the old Carthaginian inner harbours, on the right. Some say Alexandria is a bigger port and that may be true but surely no port could be busier.

We turned right two streets before we met the warehouse district and continued until we finally reached my elegant three storey town house. It once belonged to a Roman senator but had now been my home for almost forty years. I could have chosen a house further up the hill where most of the wealthy of Carthage lived but I preferred to be close to the docks. My neighbours were commercial people, successful shipping magnates mostly. Vandal nobility owned houses at the top of the hill but spent most of their time on their country estates. The Vandal allotments, as they were known, were huge estates outside the city with extensive agricultural lands, irrigated gardens, hunting grounds, and luxurious villas. All the Vandal families had one and I was no exception. However, I rarely visited mine. I was too old to hunt and had no family of my own to base there. A steward ran the estate on my behalf and delivered a healthy income to me every season. I preferred to be in the heart of the city close to the harbour. I could keep up to date with all the news from across the Vandal Sea as we call the Mediterranean these days.

In more recent times my house served as a school, mostly for the more well-to-do boys of Carthage, although there were free places for any that showed ability and a desire to learn. The school was my home, the tutors, pupils, and servants my family. I had acquired three household slaves with the house, a *majordomo* who ran the household, a cook and a young boy who did a little of everything. They all chose to stay with me as paid servants after I had granted their manumission. Forty years on the young boy now

3

ran the household and new servants cooked and cleaned. Over the years of co-existence with the Alans, the Vandals had adopted the Alan culture of having no slaves. My tutors had been born slaves and had joined me, as freedmen, in the long trek along the coast of Africa. Manius and Yannas were well educated men of good character and no little knowledge. They acted not only as the school's tutors but also as my assistants. Beyond that they were my companions with whom I could debate the latest developments and recall past events.

The group of youths that followed dutifully behind us were all pupils at the school. Their education and development gave me a much-needed purpose now that events and age had forced me to retire from the role I had performed for all my life. My half-brother and best friend had gone. He no longer needed a counsellor and protector. Over the last year we had gradually reduced our involvement in the running of state affairs leaving Hunneric and his generation of Vandal nobles to make all the important decisions. He was the old king's son but ruled, not because of that, but because he was the oldest surviving relative which was the Vandal way. To be fair the "new generation" were old men themselves by any standard but just not as ancient as the old king had been.

The funeral ceremony had been something of a disappointment for me. Gaeseric, King of the

Vandals and Alans, was a genuinely great man. I called him my brother for we had the same mother, but my father was a Roman and his was a Vandal. Gaeseric means 'Spear King' in Vandalic, a language the young generation nowadays is forgetting. Gaeseric died last week. He was 87 years old. He had ruled for fifty years and had achieved remarkable things. Ten Emperors of the Western Roman Empire had ruled since Gaeseric became king. He had Hunneric marry Eudocia the daughter of the emperor Valentinian. Of course, the Western Roman Empire was now no more and if any one man was responsible for its demise it was Gaeseric. The ceremony should have reflected that. Kings and leaders from every region should have attended and paid homage to him and his achievements but none did. Hostile relations prevailed in many areas so perhaps it was not that surprising. The coronation of the new king, Hunneric, had been an altogether grander affair with military parades and displays of wealth including some of the spoils of the great raid on Rome just over twenty years earlier. The new king threw coins to the masses lining the streets of Carthage as he passed by, aping the old traditions of a Roman triumph. Hunneric is sixty years old and he and his younger brothers and their cohort of mostly younger companions were born in Hispania or Africa. They know little of the early struggles of the Vandal migration. Hunneric's rule would be a quite different one, a prospect that worried me.

A group of young Vandal warriors, dressed in their finery and fully armoured with sword, spear and shield, strode past us, no doubt on their way to one of the harbour taverns. They had been part of the funeral honour guard. As one they called out "Hail Scuta" as they passed me. My thoughts were immediately thrown back into the past and my childhood. My name then was Marcus Flavius Eutychianus, and, of course, it still is, although I rarely have occasion to use my original Roman *tri nomina*. At home and at school I am Master Marcus to my tutors, pupils, and servants; however I have answered to another name most of my life: one given to me by the people who adopted me as a boy.

"Why do they always call out Scuta when they see you Master Marcus?" asked the youngest of the youths.

An older boy answered for me. "Don't you know anything? It's the master's Vandal name. Scuta short for Scutum – shield. Master Marcus was shield to the spear of the great king. Though I am not sure how the name came about."

6

"Even I don't know that story in full," added Yannus "and I have known Master Marcus all my life."

"We should hold a lesson on those early days of the Vandal migration. I fear the young today know nothing of the migration or how Carthage became the capital of the Vandal realm. I bet the boys don't even know where the Vandals originally come from," challenged Manius.

"I do" said one, "they came from Hispania. My grandfather told me."

There was an element of truth in what he said but it was far from the whole story.

"Didn't they come from the dark forests of Germania?" shouted another.

"How could they have come from there? It's the other side of the world," countered another.

"Surely we came across the sea. Everyone knows the Vandals rule the sea," blurted out the youngest again, "from Hispania like my grandfather said."

From their comments I could see I had been derelict in my duty to instruct the boys about their heritage. A history lesson was needed.

"Master, I think you should dictate your memoires to us. Then we can write the history of the Vandals," suggested Manius.

I would not be needed to counsel the king anymore, so the idea had appeal. The story I could tell could only be told by me. I was there with Gaeseric at the very beginning, and I was the only one to outlive him. I was with him for every step of an incredible journey. The Asding Vandals were an insignificant Germanic tribe with an undistinguished military record which saw them lose most of their battles. If any tribe were to conquer the richest province in the Roman Empire it should have been one of the major groups like the Goths who conquered Hispania or the Franks who ruled much of Gaul. That the Asding Vandals survived a great migration from Pannonia to Africa is a miracle. That they ended up becoming a sea power and ruling the Mediterranean Seas beyond belief. That they created a Vandal kingdom in North Africa so powerful they could sack Rome, incredible. My pupils needed to know how it all became possible. Even the new king, Hunneric, could benefit from a greater understanding of how his forbears created the great wealth he now enjoyed.

So the next day began a routine of spending two or three hours every morning dictating my memories to Manius whilst Yannus conducted the day's lessons. Both he and Manius were proficient in a type of shorthand notetaking that Cicero's servant, Tiro, had developed centuries earlier. Later in the day Manius would transcribe the shorthand into well-structured Latin sentences and read the words back to me. I needed them both to marshal my thoughts into some sort of chronological order as I tended to drift from one period to another. My hands are too shaky to write myself and my legs are little better.

At lunchtime we had a habit of taking a leisurely walk along to the *Mandrikon*. The central island in the old circular harbour, reached by a narrow causeway, was not for everyone. The harbour master had his office there along with his team of port tax collectors, cargo checkers and marines. The circular harbour was for *dromons*, war ships, only. Each ship had a covered wharf around the outside of the harbour. The central island had berths for up to eight ships and these were reserved for important visitors. The connecting rectangular harbour had a more mixed use but was still for the privileged: ships trading on behalf of the kingdom, warships returning with spoils or embarking on raids and the ships of the richest of the shipping community. Each day I would take up my regular station at the waterside restaurant next to the harbour master's office. I eat and drink little these days, but the steady flow of visitors, albeit fewer than there used to be, is a constant entertainment. Ship captains know where to come to find me, as do the noble Vandal leaders but unfortunately now that Gaeser, as I used to call him, was gone no one will consult me any longer. However, the ship captains still see value in reporting the news from their travels across Europe. It was what Gaeser, and I had always done. If a ship's captain had important news he was allowed to berth on the central island. It was how we knew the latest news before anyone else and could be one step ahead of our enemies. We would always reward the captains for their troubles. A waiver of port taxes was extremely valuable to them and the loss of tax insignificant to the Vandal kingdom.

On that first day after the funeral, I recognised an old friend waiting at my table by the waterside. The sailing season would not start for another month, so I knew he had not come far. Zanthi was a weathered old Carthaginian captain I had known for years. He did the rounds of the Vandal islands, Sicily, Sardinia, Corsica, and the Balearics, often bringing messages from the local governors.

"Hail Scuta, I am so sorry to hear of the passing of our great lord. I hope the funeral did the great man justice," said Zanthi.

I expressed my disappointment with the funeral arrangements and my misgivings over the prospect of Hunneric as king. I preferred to focus on other things and so asked him where he had sailed from so early in the season and what news he brought.

"I've come from Lilybaeum just across the water in Sicily. I brought tribute from Odoacer for Gaeseric as they had agreed. Of course, Hunneric's men have already been down and taken it. Anyway at least we have peace in Sicily thanks to the treaty. Aside from that, you may be interested to know there was an eastern ship in port at Lilybaeum. They carried news from Constantinople that your old friend Basiliscus has died in prison."

Basiliscus had been no friend of mine and I certainly did not mourn his passing. How the old fool had got to be the Eastern Emperor for a short while I never did understand. I told Manius and Yannas that I would tell them stories the next day about the "great" Basiliscus that they would not believe.

"No, Master. That story is quite recent, and we both recall the events ourselves. Tomorrow we must start at the beginning. Tell us about your early childhood," Manius commanded.

Chapter 1

My early childhood

My earliest memory is of my tutor, Gregor, taking us for a walk down by the river which ran past our home. We would often do this, but this particular day was recounted so frequently I am not sure if I remember it directly or if I only remember the retelling of it.

We are sitting by the riverbank. Our ever-present Vandal guard is dozing against a tree as Gregor selects a branch with which to make a fishing rod.

"Now boys, the rod needs to be about the same height as Marcus," Gregor instructed as he cut the branch down to size.

At six years old I am a tall boy of nearly four feet.

"I want to go first," demands my little brother who is two years younger and significantly smaller than me.

Gregor adopts the stern voice familiar to us from our lessons. "Gaius, you must wait your turn. Marcus is older and bigger than you. He should go first."

Only my mother and Gregor called my brother Gaius. Gregor finishes the rod with a loop to hold the waxed cord, a cork float, and a little iron hook we got from the blacksmith. "Now boys. What do fish like to eat?"

Despite the age gap my brother would often jump in first with an answer. "Worms. They like worms!"

The finished rod with float and baited hook were handed to me and the fishing began. After what seemed an age of waiting, nothing happened. My brother impatiently snatched the rod from me. "You have to get closer Marcus."

He promptly went right to the edge of the bank and immediately fell into the fast-flowing river. I jumped in after him attempting to grab him before he was carried away. Neither of us could swim but I nevertheless managed to get a hold of his tunic. As soon as I did, Gregor, a fine swimmer, was there beside us, hauling us back to the bank. The part of the story I definitely remember directly is the praise heaped on me by my stepfather. He was a hard man and praise was rare. Our guard received ten lashes of the whip for allowing the Vandal princeling to nearly drown. We both watched the punishment with fascination. He would never guard us again. My mother, quite rightly, praised the real hero, Gregor.

Our childhood home was close to a great city. A city that was in fact an Imperial capital. For over one hundred years Sirmium had been one of the four Imperial capitals of the Roman Empire along with Constantinople, Mediolanum, and Augusta

Treverom. Significantly it was also the capital of the *praetorian prefecture* of Illyricum and Pannonia Secunda. Significant because my father, my real father, had been *praetorian prefect* for a brief period. Now while that sounds important, it was merely a figurehead position with little power. Others held the real power in the region at that time. In earlier times the Roman *praetorian prefect* was a military man with the power to govern his *prefecture* as he saw fit. By the time my father held the office it was purely an administrative position granted to those in favour with the court in Constantinople. Illyricum was a part of the Eastern half of the Empire in that period and only later transferred to the West. However, my father received the posting not because he was in favour but because he was in serious political trouble. This was all before I was born, of course, and naturally my knowledge of events, as related to me by my mother, Flavia, and by Gregor, are a little sketchy.

"Your father and I were not together for very long," my mother recounted. "Our marriage was arranged very quickly because your father was on the wrong side of a court intrigue in Constantinople and had to get out of the city quickly. Things would have gone badly for him if the powerful Goth faction in the city had not protected him. You see, ever since the devastating battle of Adrianople the Goths have been a hugely influential tribal people within the Eastern Empire. The Goths were at the time of your father's political difficulties, in the process of taking *de facto* control of Illyricum and Pannonia and it suited their purposes to have a compliant Roman *prefect*. So they chose your father. I was just fifteen when we travelled here and within a year your father had died, and I was pregnant with you. Thank God I had my ladies and Gregor to look after me."

My father, also Marcus Flavius Eutychianus, moved to Sirmium in 388 when he was well into his forties and, by most standards, an old man. I was born that year in the Imperial palace that dominated the centre of the city. As was traditional I took my father's name. I have no memory of either my father or the Imperial palace. After the sudden death of my father, my mother, her assistants, and Gregor moved out of the Imperial palace to the summer palace just across the river outside the city. My mother told me we moved there for security reasons after the Roman garrison had abandoned the city under constant pressure from various raiding Goth factions and riotous locals. The summer palace was a huge building complex with every manner of amenities and was a self-contained community. The emperor Gratian had grown up there. Regardless of the various attractions the crucial factor in our moving there was the presence of 500 troopers of a squadron, an *ala*, of Vandal cavalry stationed within the grounds.

My early childhood had everything a boy could want. A loving mother and a strict but fair stepfather whom we were both inspired to emulate. There were many young children living in the palace grounds the result of liaisons between the young Vandal troopers and the locals. However we were the only two children to live inside the palace and we were the only ones, plus later a few select others, to receive a classic Roman education from the two Greek tutors who lived with us. Initially there had only been Gregor, who had been my mother's tutor when she had travelled from Constantinople. My maternal grandfather had insisted his daughter have a tutor as a part of the marriage contract. Gregor taught us to read and write in Latin and to speak the language properly. We did arithmetic and learnt to measure, weigh, and count. My brother learnt at a similar level to me despite being two years younger. Everyone acknowledged him as an extremely bright child.

My brother had blond hair like so many of the Vandal troopers and indeed like my stepfather. It was clear to everyone who his father was. Nevertheless, my mother, for reasons unclear to me, insisted on giving him the Roman name Gaius. No doubt she feared some sort of social judgement and thought to protect him from gossip. Or alternatively she wanted to link him to my uncle who went by that name and was becoming increasingly prominent in Constantinople. My stepfather, of course, rejected that name and always called my brother Gisselitta, Little Arrow. You see, my stepfather was Godigsel, Great Arrow, of the Asding Vandal royal family. So it was that the baby who would become known to the world as Gaeseric, King of the Vandals and Alans, was christened twice. Firstly, with all formal ceremony by the catholic Bishop of Sirmium, with the Roman name Gaius. Then a little later he was christened again with the Vandal name Gisselitta. The Vandal troopers had their own small wooden church next to the barracks where a trooper called Ulfred led services in the Arian Christian creed. It was the catholic church who applied the term Arian to their beliefs, to the Vandals they were simply Christian. Ulfred, and the Vandals who had converted to Christianity, followed the teaching of Wulfila, the man who had brought Christianity to the Goths and had translated the bible into Gothic.

Godigsel would later have the Roman rank of *prefectus* as commander of the *ala*. However, when we first arrived at the summer palace, Godigsel's father, Gibamundus, had been *prefectus*. It cannot have surprised many that, after my father, the Roman *pretorian prefect,* had passed away, his young wife should have become attached to the commander's son. Godigsel was then a dashing young *decurion*, a commander of thirty troopers. Gibamundus subsequently retired to the Vandal homelands alongside the Tisza River on the other side of the Danube and ruled there as one of two kings.

Shortly after Godigsel became *prefectus* we had a visit from his son by his first marriage. Gunderic was eighteen at that time, eager to visit his father and stepbrother and experience life with the *ala*. He brought a group of friends with him, and they all made a great fuss of little Gisselitta. Godigsel persuaded one of Gunderic's friends, Axxa, to stay and be Gisselitta's personal guard.

Axxa had grown up by the River Tisza in Patiscum, the main town of the Vandal homelands. He knew how to swim, to ride, to hunt, to fight and above all to laugh. We adored him and he would watch over us for many years. Before long, our visits to the river with Gregor and Axxa involved swimming races across the Sava and back. Axxa would always be first and Gregor always last, deliberately holding back just in case Gisselitta got into difficulties.

Axxa took over all our physical education, be it riding lessons or weapons training. When I was nine he persuaded Godigsel that we were big enough to ride an Alan horse as all the troopers did. I was not sure my brother was big enough but there was no way I could have a new horse if Gisselitta did not have one too.

My stepfather needed little excuse to visit his good friend Asphax, the leader of the Sava River Alans. At the Alan camp Asphax and his son, Tzason, greeted us warmly in Vandalic.

"Godigsel my old friend it is good to see you and your boys again. Let Tzason here, take the boys to the horse herds while you and I have a drink and reminisce that glorious night at the Fridgid River, when we both got rich."

Asphax laughed aloud and walked away slapping Godigsel's back. When Tzason mimicked his father's actions behind his back we all laughed too. Tzason was Gisselitta's age, and we liked him immediately. A huge Alano hound followed him everywhere obeying his every command. I could see Gisselitta wanted a dog like that.

An Alan warrior called Safrax took us to the horse herds and supervised the selection. He quickly identified two suitable horses from the thirty or forty in the herd and Axxa was happy to nod his agreement.

Tzason pointed to a horse and said, "Now watch this Gisselitta. This one will be yours."

Tzason rode out into the horse herd whirling his lasso. He caught the horse with his first throw and promptly trotted back. Tzason dismounted and placed a crab apple into Gisselitta's hand and a simple rope halter onto the horse.

"Come and say hello to your new horse Gisselitta."

19

Tzason whispered in the horse's ear and blew gently up his nose as Gisselitta offered the crab apple. Tzason made to lift my brother up, but the horse backed away. Gisselitta hesitated, there was no saddle and the animal seemed too big for him. Tzason, although no bigger than my brother, leaped onto the horse and held his arm out for Axxa to lift Gisselitta up in front of him. The two boys cantered around the field laughing all the way. After one circuit of the field they returned whereupon Tzason jumped off leaving Gisselitta to ride his new horse alone. Returning to the herd, Tzason soon lassoed the horse Safrax had picked out for me.

After that time we made regular visits to the Alan camp, and it was always a fun event. The camp was never in the same place as they moved every season, but it was always somewhere along the Sava River. There were over a thousand warriors at the camp, and it was a quite different affair to the Vandal barracks at the summer palace. Although several Alan bands formed cavalry *alae* for the Roman army, both in the West and in the East, the Sava valley Alans were allied quite closely to Alaric's Goths and generally fought alongside them. The camp was a vast sea of tents around a large corral of wagons. The fields around were filled with herds of goats, cows, and oxen along with hundreds of grazing horses. The Alans bred horses and were renowned for their horse handling skills. They were suppliers of fine mounts to any who had the money to buy, and all the Vandals' horses came from the Alan camp. They also bred large Alano dogs and trained them for different tasks. Some shepherded animals, some were used to hunt but the most prized were the ferocious war dogs. At every visit they would put on a display of horsemanship for our entertainment. Boys and, to our amazement, girls of our age would ride past standing on a horse's back or whirling a lasso to catch another horse. Alans began to ride as soon as they could walk. They used no stirrup and only a remarkably simple harness. Their incredible riding skills had to be seen to be believed. The warriors could fire an arrow from a galloping horse facing forwards or backwards. The best display was the practise of their trademark attack. Twenty Alan horsemen would gallop towards a target, release their throwing spears in unison and wheel away as if they were one body leaving the target looking like a porcupine. In a real battle there would have been wave after wave of such attacks with hundreds of warriors.

Later, when we were a gang of eight, Gisselitta made Tzason coach us on galloping in line, throwing our wooden javelins and turning away together. I admit that I was not the only one to fall from his pony in the act of throwing. Nevertheless, our horse-riding skills did improve.

Of course, every visit to the Alan camp would end in a great feast. Before we could eat, the Alans would kneel as one around a golden sword. I never quite understood what the Alan religion was, but whatever it was, the golden sword seemed to be at the centre of their beliefs.

It was Axxa who organised our first trip to the Sirmium hippodrome for the chariot races. Godigsel was reluctant to allow it because of the regular outbreaks of violence at the games. However lots of off-duty troopers wanted to go so it was not difficult to arrange a guard detail to protect us. Our guards all supported the green team, so we did too.

The city's garrison at that time comprised mostly men from the Quadi tribe. We sat next to Vangio, the commander of the Quadi auxiliaries, and his son, Fredobodus. Fredo, as we would come to call him, was a huge boy about a year older than me.

"We are supporting the greens," we told him.

He gave an inane grin and said, "Me too, and so do the rest of the garrison, but my father supports the whites because he wants to suck up to the rich nobles."

Most of the city's population supported the blues and the blues usually won. Vangio was briefly delighted when the whites won and then realised that, as the blues had not won, there would be a riot and his men would have to deal with the aftermath. The greens came last, but it didn't detract from the most thrilling experience of my young life.

I could see that Yannus and Manius had questions. Yannus' was understandable. He had been mistreated as a young slave before he came to join my *familia,* and he could not accept my seemingly idyllic childhood.

"Master were you never beaten when you were young? I know you grew up in a palace but surely there must have been beatings!"

There were, of course, beatings. They tend not to stick in the memory quite so vividly. My stepfather beat us for any misdemeanour. Usually it was Gisselitta causing mischief for which we would both be beaten. Gregor would rap our hands with a cane if we failed to pay attention in class. Axxa would smack his wooden sword into our backs if we made the wrong sword stroke during weapons training and my mother would give us a verbal beating if we used vulgar Latin in the palace.

Manius' question struck a different tone. "Master, you are one of the most knowledgeable men I know. I cannot understand how you could have acquired so much knowledge during the disruption of the great migration. From what you say, Gregor's lessons were limited to the basics of a Roman education. Who taught you the history, the literature, the poetry, the rhetoric, the philosophy, and the logic I know you have studied?"

One man was responsible for that as I shall explain.

Chapter 2

My education

Later in the Autumn of the year when we acquired our new horses, our education changed abruptly. We were in our schoolroom pretending to listen to Gregor drone on about Latin grammar. Our thoughts were on the ride down the river we had been promised by Axxa.

Our new Alan mounts were ready waiting outside when a band of Goths rode into the palace grounds causing a panic in the barracks. We raced to the window to observe as the Vandal troopers hurriedly turned out to meet them.

"Those Goth boys look about your age Marcus," observed Gisselitta.

There were, indeed, three young boys amongst the Goths and their leader pointed to them as he spoke to Godigsel before gesturing towards the covered wagon that slowly trundled into the compound. The Goths left before we could find out more, leaving the young Goths and the wagon behind. My stepfather brought the Goth boys into the classroom and announced that they had brought a present from the great Goth leader, Alaric.

"Was that Alaric in the compound?" my brother blurted out.

The oldest Goth boy responded. "No, that was my father, Athaulf. He is also a great leader. Alaric is my uncle. I am Indulf of the Trevingi Goths."

The present was an old Greek man who they claimed was a famous teacher, a *grammaticus*. Diomedes hobbled into the room with the aid of a stick. He stroked his long grey beard and nodded to us all. We would grow to love him dearly for he was an extremely learned man and he opened up a whole new world of knowledge for us.

We later learnt that he had been taken in a Goth raid on Athens and he did, indeed, have some renown in that city as both a teacher and philosopher. His wagon contained a veritable library of scrolls containing the works of both Greek and Roman philosophers, historians, and playwrights. From that point onwards we studied the great works of literature in Greek and Latin, poetry, philosophy, rhetoric and, of particular interest to my brother, history. We learnt, and later re-enacted with the local boys, every great battle from Greek and Roman history. The campaigns of Alexander the Great were a particular fascination for my brother. He dreamed of conquering the world with a band of companions and of riding a magnificent black horse just like Alexander had.

Although Gisselitta and I benefited greatly from the 'gift' of Diomedes, he had not been brought to educate us. He had been brought to continue the education of Indulf and his cousins. From that point onwards the three Goth boys stayed with us every winter returning home to their families in the Summer. Indulf was the oldest and my age. Trasovado and Coccas were twins and a year younger. Their fathers wanted the boys to receive a Roman education, the better to achieve high ranks in the Roman army. When the Goths moved back into Pannonia after a few years in Greece, Alaric decided that the summer palace was a more suitable base for the *grammaticus* than a Goth campsite. Alaric also wanted to promote relations with the Vandal troops whom he wished to have as allies. Very soon the reputation of Diomedes' school at the summer palace spread around the region.

After some negotiation between Godigsel and their fathers three more boys joined the school the following year. Fredo, whom we knew from the chariot races, was the oldest at fifteen and, by far, the biggest. We were in awe of his strength and boxing ability. He would delight in outboxing the younger Vandal troopers even though he was younger than they were. Fredo struggled a little with the lessons and it was usually young Gisselitta who helped him along.

Ingamar was fourteen and such were his good looks that he drew stares from both men and women in the marketplace. He could sail a ketch and regularly took us on fishing trips down the Sava River which ran past the palace. He had been brought up on the Roman river galleys on the Danube. His father was the *prefectus* of the Pannonian *classis* or fleet. He commanded the Alemanni river frontier troops, *ripenses*, who manned the fleet based at Taurunum across the estuary from Singidunum, where the Sava met the Danube.

When the familiar face of Tzason of the Alans joined our group, we were all delighted. He entertained us all with constant pranks and jokes. The tricks he could perform on his pony were unbelievable. He could rise up from sitting on his horse to standing and then down again.

"If you think that's good you should see my younger sister. She can jump from one horse to another."

Tzason loved to wrestle, as did all the Alans, and was easily the best wrestler in our group. He brought his Alano dog with him along with an Alano puppy as a gift for Gisselitta. Tzason's dog was called Shirkar, which I believe meant hunter in Alanic, and the huge beast was indeed a formidable hunter and could take down a small deer given the chance. Gisselitta named his dog Wolf and delighted in training the dog to obey commands. Tzason thought that Wolf would be big enough to be a war dog when fully grown.

Tzason's father, Asphax, was the leader of the Sava River Alans but, unlike with the other boys, there was no presumption that Tzason would lead in due course. The Alans chose the best warrior as leader regardless of family ties. We boys became good friends and in the early stages Gisselitta, as the youngest, was not the leader. Fredo and Ingamar were older, but Indulf had a confidence and arrogance about him that meant we all accepted that he was the natural leader of our little gang.

There was plenty of room in the palace for us all to have a room, but our mother thought it best we shared two to a room. The pairings came naturally as Gisselitta and I were used to sharing, as were the twins. When the two Suebic boys, Ingamar and Fredo, agreed to share, it left Indulf and Tzason together. I was concerned that there might be friction between the two, but I was wrong. They formed a close bond based on their mutual experience of being the sons of great leaders.

Axxa was not happy with the arrangements. None of the boys' fathers had thought to send bodyguards. He now had a group of eight to look after. Each Autumn, after the harvest was in, we received new recruits from the Vandal homelands. At the same time some of the veterans would choose to retire to the Tisza valley. That year we had a surplus of recruits over retirees and Axxa determined to select the best to join our guards. Axxa knew Wada and Otte from Patiscum. After they had passed on news from the homeland, Axxa offered them a place in our guard. Wada's father was one of Gibamudus' oathsworn and a renowned warrior. Otte's father was the town blacksmith. Otte had already learnt much of his father's trade but yearned for a little adventure before he settled to a working life. Both Wada and Otte jumped at the chance to have the honour of being bodyguard to the Vandal princeling and his friends.

Axxa wanted more than two extra guards and subjected the other new recruits to vigorous tests of riding, fighting, and swimming before making his selection. They all came from villages to the south of the Tisza valley. Ulli's father was a carpenter and, much like Otte, had already absorbed a lot of his father's skills. He could make spear shafts and shields but wanted to see a little of the world before he settled to family life in the village. Skara had excellent riding skills and loved to be around horses. Kitan was the best swimmer having grown up beside the river. His father operated a ferry across the Tisza, and Kitan was able to sail a small boat up to Patiscum on market days. The new recruits quickly formed a bond between themselves, following Axxa's every command.

Our lessons now had an intensity we were not used to. The Goth boys had a good understanding of Diomedes' methods having already studied with him for two years when the Goths were based in Epirus, northern Greece. Diomedes knew he would spark a reaction when he initiated a discussion of one of the most important battles of recent times. Our *grammaticus* said he did not need scrolls to know what happened as he had spoken to people who had been there. Indulf responded with characteristic arrogance.

"My father was there and so was the twins' father."

The Battle of Adrianople in 378 was undoubtably the Goths' greatest victory and the boys must have heard the story retold a hundred times around the Goth campfires. The insight that Diomedes wanted to convey was that it was an event that changed Roman history for ever. Led by Alaric's predecessor, Fritigern who was Indulf's grandfather, the forces of the Tervingi Goths and other allied tribes had destroyed the Eastern Empire's field army of 20,000 men. The emperor Valens had been killed during the fighting.

Tzason was not to be outdone by the Goth boys.

"My father was also there, and he says that it was the Alan cavalry attack on the flanks of the legions that had decided the battle."

Diomedes settled matters by declaring that the decisive cavalry attack had comprised both Goths and Alans. Our teacher emphasized the political consequences of the battle telling us that for the first time in Roman history, a "barbarian" tribe had entered the Empire and settled on the land under their own leadership and the Romans simply had to accept it.

Our next lesson was on the origins of the Alans. I believe Tzason learnt as much as we did even though he had grown up listening to all the myths, legends, and stories of his people. Diomedes took us right back to their origins.

"They may have been one ethnic group in their early beginnings in the East. Nobody knows. They were nomadic people living on the wide-open plains of the steppes."

"That's where our love of horses comes from," interrupted Tzason.

Diomedes continued. "They constantly waged war on their neighbours and often assimilated with the tribes they conquered. They abhorred slavery, and captured prisoners were given a chance to prove themselves in battle fighting for the Alans. If they were successful, they could become Alan by adopting the culture and practices of that band. Captured children were brought up as Alan children and were accepted as full members of the band. So over time the ethnic mix became confused, but the culture and way of life and war was distinctly Alan."

Tzason interrupted again. "It's true, we never keep slaves. And we don't look any different from Goths or Vandals. Not like the Huns. Now they do look different."

Diomedes tried to draw Gisselitta into the discussion.

"The Alan ability to assimilate easily was crucial for the Vandals. The Asding Vandal homelands along the Tisza River in Pannonia are shared with Samartian Iazyges and various bands of Alans. The Alans merged with the Samartians long ago and have always mixed easily with the Vandals. The Asding Vandals learnt the value of mounted warfare from the Alans, and, unlike most Germanic tribes, Asding Vandals rarely fight on foot, I believe."

Gisselitta responded as Diomedes hoped he would.

"My father told me that the Siling Vandals that live to the north of the mountains don't have many horses. Only rich Siling nobles fight on a horse. We Asdings used to be the same until we migrated south to the Tisza valley. By living alongside the Alans we had access to a constant supply of horses, and we learnt how to fight from horseback."

Diomedes had a copy of a book titled, *Contra Alanos*, written by a Roman general called Arrian which described in detail the Alans' highly effective fighting tactics and how to counter them. I saw those tactics first-hand, exactly as Arrian described, several times during the great migration and very thankful for them I was too. It seems from the earliest of times the Romans were aware of the fighting prowess of the Alans and of the qualities of their steppe ponies. As we knew from our visits to the Sava valley camp, the Alans bred their own horses. They were smaller than Roman horses but more nimble and much hardier. They had great endurance and Alan bands could cover large distances quickly by each warrior having a second horse to replace a tiring mount.

For all the excitement the lessons created for the Goth boys and Tzason, Gisselitta and the Suebic boys were less impressed. The absence of gr eat Vandal victories from our history lessons was probably what caused Gisselitta's obsession with both Hannibal and Alexander the Great.

After our lesson with Diomedes on the Punic Wars, we were all amazed when Gisselitta the next day engaged our *grammaticus* in a debate on the positives and negatives of Hannibal's long campaign.

My brother declared, "Hannibal's route over the Alps with his elephants was a brilliant strategy even though he lost many men and animals in the mountains. He took the Romans by surprise and showed great judgment in recruiting the support of the Hispanic and Celtic tribes to join his army. His Numidian cavalry could launch fast missile attacks just like the Alans. There was no debating that he was a great general, perhaps the greatest, as demonstrated by his victories at Cannae and Lake Trasimene. But his big mistake was not taking Rome and finishing the war when he had the Romans on their knees."

"A telling point young master. Maybe one day you will have the opportunity to correct Hannibal's mistake," joked Diomedes by way of bringing the debate to an end.

None could have predicted the prescience of Diomedes' remark.

Outside lessons in our mock fights, however, Gisselitta always wanted to be Alexander and wanted us to be Alexander's legendary companions. Tzason would play along and promised to find Gisselitta a black horse with a white flash on its head, just like Alexander's Bucephalus. Gisselitta was too young to lead at that stage and, despite his prompting, we usually went along with what Indulf wanted to do.

Gisselitta and I spoke Latin within the home with my mother and my mother's personal household assistants and, of course, our lessons were in Latin with a little Greek. Amongst ourselves we spoke the vulgar Latin of the streets as did the local Pannonians in our community. To the horror of my mother we could mimic the local accents perfectly. A few Illyrians lived in the community, and amongst themselves, they had their own impenetrable language.

When we were doing weapons training in the barracks, we spoke Vandalic. The Vandals and the Goths could understand each other's languages without too much difficulty and the local Alans spoke Gothic like native speakers. No-one attempted to speak the strange sounding Alanic language that Tzason spoke amongst his own people. The newly arrived Vandal troopers who formed our bodyguard explained that there were villages in the homelands where the Samartian Iazyges people spoke a form of Alanic. The Quadi, Marcomanni and Alemanni were all tribes of the Suebic federation in Germania and spoke similar languages. The Vandals and Goths used many similar words to the Suebi but meaningful conversation between the two groups was difficult.

Towards the end of our time at the summer palace, after we had suffered many upheavals and adventures together, the Goths brought another youth to join our lessons. His name was Aetius, and he was a highborn Roman held as a hostage by Alaric. I immediately felt I should put myself forward as his protector and translator but then looked foolish as he greeted Godigsel with great deference in fluent Gothic. He needed no protection either as he quickly demonstrated skills with both words and weapons. He was brave enough to take on Fredo in boxing and Tzason at wrestling and, whilst he lost both bouts, he did well enough to earn applause from everyone. I admit I was a little jealous of Aetius and I feared he would disrupt our little group. My brother, on the other hand, spent every available minute talking with the Roman youth and they became fast friends. My fears subsided when, after only two months, the Goths came and took Aetius back to Alaric.

When we boys got bored of our enclosed community and the daily routines there would always be a trip away or a grand visit from someone important to bring us excitement. For military, political, and social reasons Godigsel liked to keep in regular contact with our neighbours, particularly the Alans as they provided all the horses for the *ala*. Whenever we left the confines of the palace, we had our guard of Axxa and his five young Vandal troopers. Nevertheless, it gave us the freedom to go into town and experience the excitement of the chariot races at the hippodrome on a regular basis.

As young adolescents we listened eagerly to the stories of the young Vandal troopers who spent their leave experiencing the delights of the port of Singidunum. Our jealousy was made worse when Ingamar told us of his own adventures in the port after sailing across the estuary in his little ketch. We longed for the time when we would be allowed to ride down to the river at Taurunum on our own or even to go into Sirmium and explore the city without our constant shadows. Our life experiences in the city would have to wait for the time being but our political education was just about to begin.

At this point I could see Yannus was bursting to interrupt. I nodded to him, and his question tumbled out.

"The Roman hostage Aetius, was he the famous Aetius who defeated Attila at the battle of Catalaunian Fields in Vandal year 12? They say he saved the Western Roman Empire that day."

I confirmed that it was. After the Goths released him, he became a hostage of the Huns. The experiences he gained and the languages he learnt while a hostage of the Goths and the Huns were vital to his later success. His personal bodyguard, *bucellarii,* were Hunnic troops and the support of the Huns was crucial to his rise to become *de facto* ruler of the Western Roman Empire. Quite ironic when you remember that it was Aetius who defeated Attila and brought down the Hun Empire.

Chapter 3

Alaric and the Trevingi Goths

For Gisselitta, the events of 401 dictated that Godigsel would begin the political education of his son. I was not to be excluded. We thought we had understood from Diomedes' lessons that Alaric of the Trevingi Goths was the most powerful man in our province. We were aware that Alaric was *magister militum per Illyricum*, commander of all forces in Illyria and, as such, in overall command of our Vandal *ala*. However, it was only after Indulf's father, Athaulf, rode into the summer palace in early Spring that year and the events that followed, that the extent of his power truly struck home. Athaulf rode with his oathsworn warriors, which included the father of the twins, Trasovado and Coccas. We naturally assumed the fathers were visiting their sons. However, the urgency of the situation quickly became apparent when Athaulf dispensed with the usual ritual greetings to begin immediate discussions with Godigsel. Indulf was able to persuade his father that he should attend, along with Tzason. Gisselitta asked Godigsel if he too could attend, and whilst it was obvious our stepfather disapproved, he nevertheless felt obliged to agree. This meant, as always, that I too would be included.

Athaulf began. "All the leaders of the different Goth tribes are meeting to decide how to respond to the massacre of our people in Constantinople last year."

Indulf whispered to us, "I told you there was a massacre of Goths in the east." We had not believed him at the time, but Diomedes had been able to confirm, from different sources, that a change of regime in the eastern capital had resulted in a purge of every Goth in the city. The rumour was that seven thousand Goths had died.

Athaulf continued, "We will choose an overall leader of the Goths so that, whatever we decide to do, we do as one people."

Godigsel asked, "I thought your brother-in-law was secure in his position as leader. Is Alaric challenged?"

"Saurus, a member of the royal Amal dynasty of the Greuthungi Goths, has a lot of support."

We knew from the Goth boys that the Greuthungi were the other major grouping of Goths and that there was no love lost between the Trevingi and the Greuthungi.

Godigsel looked concerned. "Can Saurus win?"

Athaulf admitted that the decision could go either way.

"This is why I am here. Alaric has already received the backing of the Alans, and Asphax will be at the meeting to support him. Charaton of the Huns has also confirmed his backing. Alaric commands you, Godigsel, to come to the meeting and pledge the support of the Vandals."

Godigsel was shocked but tried not to show it. He responded in the only way he felt he could.

"I will come, and I will support Alaric, but you know I cannot speak for my father and the Vandals across the river."

Indulf spoke out for the first time.

"Father, I will travel to the meeting and help you support Uncle Alaric."

Athaulf seemed pleased with this and gestured to Tzason and Gisselitta.

"The presence of the sons of the leaders would create a good impression. Bring the boys with you."

So it was that we joined Athaulf, Asphax and Godigsel with their personal bodyguards travelling to the great Goth gathering. We boys were all in a high state of excitement to be included in such a great adventure. Godigsel, on the other hand, was a worried man, appearing to have the weight of the world on his shoulders. He told us, in no uncertain terms, to ride at the rear of the group with our own Vandal guards. We all did as we were told. All that is except for Indulf, who rode alongside Athaulf at the head of the column. Indulf adopted the pose of a Goth warrior, and we were all impressed.

At the first encampment we came across, we saw the strangest people we had ever encountered. The warriors had dark skins and noses squashed flat. They wore funny conical hats with tassels hanging down. Their heads appeared strangely elongated, and their hair was black with long braided tails down their backs. The Goths and Vandals mostly had beards, yet these people had no facial hair just a few wispy strands on their chins. When they stood to greet Athaulf we noticed how short they all seemed, but they also had broad chests with muscular arms. They wore clothes made from animal skins, mostly sheepskin, and spoke a guttural form of Gothic to Athaulf. The majority seemed indifferent to our presence and continued squatting on their haunches in small groups. Traso confirmed our suspicions.

"These are Huns. They fought with us at Adrianople and were part of the Goth raids on Greece. They are mercenaries and will fight for whoever promises the most money. You should never trust them, but you must acknowledge they are great fighters. They ride as well as any Alan and just look at their horse herds. Superb animals."

Tzason made similar complimentary comments on the quality of the Huns' horse herds as we passed by. Our horses were similar and, whilst we appreciated their qualities of strength and endurance, we saw no beauty in them. To us they appeared small, ugly, shaggy haired, bony creatures. Gisselitta was sure that Alexander had not ridden an Alan or Hun horse.

We rode past three more encampments and at each one Traso and Coccas explained which Goth band we were passing. I cannot remember the names of the different tribes. That none were the Trevingi or the Greuthungi was evident when we approached the centre of the Goth gathering. A small hill divided two vast tent cities with wagon corrals in their centre.

Traso gestured to the right. "Behold, our people, the mighty Trevingi."

"And, that hoard of scum over there are the Greuthungi," Coccas sneered.

Whilst Asphax and Godigsel were taken to pay homage to Alaric, we Vandals and Alans were allocated an area to camp. Slaves were sent to serve us food and drink. A little while later Traso came to take Gisselitta, Tzason and me to meet Alaric. Indulf introduced us to the great man with a grand flourish.

"Uncle may I present my great friends, Gisselitta of the Vandals, and Tzason of the Alans. This other is the Roman boy adopted by Godigsel."

Indulf meant no insult to me, and I took none. It was simply the way things were. Indulf's true feelings became apparent when we were cornered by a group of Goth boys on our way back to our camp. After hurling racial insults at us it looked as if we would have to fight our way back. I remember wishing that Fredo was with us. Before anyone could get hurt, Indulf appeared with Traso and Coccas on either side of him. They stood in front of us confronting the Goth boys.

"Know me, Greuthungi dogs, for I am Indulf, son of Athaulf, of the Trevingi." He pointed to us and then to his cousins. "These are my brothers, and I would give my life to protect them. Who dares threaten my brothers?"

The Greuthungi boys melted away without a word.

The next day in the lee of the central hill, where a natural amphitheatre formed, the elders of all the different tribes met and held discussions for the entire day. Late in the afternoon, the senior elder of the Trevingi announced that the elders would now hear proposals from the leadership contenders. The surrounding hillsides quickly filled until there was no room to spare. The atmosphere was bubbling with anticipation and reminded me of the moment before the first chariot race at the hippodrome. It soon became apparent that there were to be only two contenders with each one introduced to the gathering by a second.

"I am Sigirus of the Greuthungi royal clan, the Amal. Some of you will remember that my brother and I fought at Adrianople. Many of you will have been with us when we raided in Greece and Macedonia. The Goths have no greater warrior than my brother Saurus whom I nominate for leader."

"I am Saurus. Accept me as leader and I will bring great wealth to us all without having to bleed the lives of our young men in the Romans' internal wars. I was there when my rival, Alaric, allowed the Eastern Emperor to sacrifice our warriors at the Fridgid River. The Eastern Empire betrayed us then and betrayed us again when they massacred our brothers in Constantinople. They are our enemies, and we must never again fight for them. We need rich farmland to feed our people. Already we can see our numbers here are exhausting the countryside of food. I propose we approach Stilico and the Western Empire and negotiate land in northern Italy for the families to settle. There will be paid employment in Stilico's armies for our young warriors. The Eastern Empire will eventually come against us if we remain here. The Western forces are weak, and we will be able to dominate their forces without having to fight a major conflict."

A huge roar greeted Saurus' words from the far side of the hill where the Greuthungi stood, but many more sections remained silent.

"I am Athaulf, son of Fritigern, of the Trevingi royal clan, the Balti. My father led our armies at Adrianople. Both my brother-in-law and I fought in that great victory. We also fought at the Fridgid River where we lost so many friends. It was my

45

brother-in-law who saved us then by forcing us to combine. It will be my brother-in-law who will save us now. I nominate Alaric."

Alaric stood to massive acclaim. Physically smaller and less imposing than Saurus, there was nevertheless an indefinable quality about the man as he waited for the gathering to calm down.

"You know who I am and what I have done," he began. "Yes, we were betrayed at the Fridgid River and yes, it was I who led you all, both Trevingi and Greuthungi, to vengeance. Who here has not become rich in gold and slaves after we conquered Macedonia and Greece? I have proved myself a good leader for all Goths and all the other tribes that follow us. I have here today Asphax of the Sava River Alans who fought with us at Adrianople. Stand Asphax."

Asphax rose. "I follow Alaric and acknowledge his leadership. The Alans will not follow Saurus."

"I have here today Charaton of the Huns who were also at Adrianople. Stand Charaton."

Charaton rose. "We follow Alaric."

"I have here today Godigsel of the Vandals. It is true that in times past we Goths fought against the Vandals, but Godigsel's father is King of the Vandals across the river and the Vandals will support us in the campaign I am about to propose."

Godigsel stood up and said, "I confirm it is so."

Gisselitta looked at me and pulled a face of utter shock.

Alaric continued, "I agree with Saurus on many issues. I agree we cannot stay where we are. I agree the Eastern Empire will eventually send armies against us. I agree we need rich farmland to feed our people and that northern Italy can provide it. I agree with Saurus that the Western forces are weak. Where we differ is that I don't propose to ask the Romans for land, I propose to take the land we want. I don't propose to join Stilico's armies, I propose to defeat them. I propose to invade Italy, and with the help of our allies the Alans, Huns, and the Vandals, create a Gothic kingdom and, what is more, I will be King of the Goths. Are you with me?"

I have no idea how many Goths were there to roar their support for Alaric, but the noise was overwhelming. It was clear Alaric had won the election and now we fully understood the power he held.

As we wandered back to our camp we pondered all that had been said in the leadership speeches and tried to reconcile it with what we knew from Diomedes' lessons and our fathers' stories.

Tzason questioned what Asphax had told him. "My father says the battle of the Fridgid River was his greatest triumph. The tribe won great riches and lost very few warriors."

Gisselitta agreed, "My father says much the same. I think the Vandals and the Alans captured the enemy baggage train."

Indulf, Traso and Coccas couldn't believe their ears.

"It was a disaster," Indulf burst out.

He let Traso begin the story of the Goth experience of the great battle seven years before.

"All the Goths in this region fought for the emperor Theodosius in the civil war against Eugenius, the Western usurper. We were required to. We were too young, of course, but every one of our older relatives were there. We have heard all the stories from those that survived. With all respect to your fathers, the Alans and the Vandals were merely scouts supporting the army flanks. It was a Goth dominated army supported by a few thousand Eastern Roman soldiers that fought the battle."

Coccas continued. "Theodosius deliberately exposed our men to slaughter by throwing them recklessly against the Western lines on the first day of the battle. He wanted to defeat the usurper, but he also wanted to weaken the Goth tribes at the same time. We lost 10,000 men that day, most of them Trevingi, including many from our own family. It was a devastating blow for our tribe."

Indulf brought the story round to the leadership contest we had just witnessed. "The battle was won on the second day but afterwards many amongst our tribe questioned Alaric's leadership. The surviving Goths had not gained as much booty from the battle as they felt their sacrifices deserved.

My uncle, Alaric, as the leader of the largest military force in the Eastern Empire, expected an official position in the Eastern Army – a position that would yield prestige, money, and grain supplies for his people – however, it was not forthcoming. Goth discontent only increased when it became known that the Vandals and Alans had gained vast amounts of treasure by capturing the baggage train of the Western Army after the battle."

"But this was all seven years ago," Gisselitta interrupted.

Indulf was able to explain. "After the battle, Alaric needed to take action to secure his position within the Trevingi Goths. He decided a successful campaign would bring him the support of his own tribe as well as the Greuthungi and other Goth bands. The target for the campaign was the man we all blamed for our losses – Theodosius. As you know, in January 395, and before our campaign could begin, Theodosius died. Nevertheless, the combined Goth armies marched on Constantinople in the Spring in open revolt against the Eastern Empire. When we reached the city I can still remember seeing the massive walls for the first time. It was impossible to attack such defences. They were simply too formidable. We turned back and ravaged Macedonia before splitting into different bands to pillage Greece. My father led the Goth forces which captured Athens taking large

49

numbers of captives. These, of course, included our *grammaticus*, Diomedes."

"So did this solve the leadership problem for your uncle?" Gisselitta queried.

"It did for a time. We stayed in Epirus for several years and that is where we began to have lessons with Diomedes. Alaric got his official appointment and there was grain and gold from the Eastern Empire. We moved back to Pannonia last year and it was only when the news came of the massacre of Goths in Constantinople that the whole leadership question came to a head again. Most of the Goths that died were Greuthungi, and, when the Romans stopped our grain deliveries, Saurus and Sigirus started to agitate for action. My uncle was forced to call all the tribes together and seek support from your fathers."

Yannus was clearly confused. "If the Goths were an independent force within the Eastern Empire, why did they have to fight for Theodosius at the Fridgid River?"

Although the Battle of Adrianople had been an overwhelming Goth victory, the subsequent Goth wars produced no clear result, despite numerous clashes, for either the Eastern Empire or for the Goths. A treaty in 382 gave both sides the opportunity to recover. Alaric led the Trevingi Goths to Pannonia where they became familiar to us in the summer palace community as the dominant force in the region. Asphax followed with his Alan band to live close to us along the Sava River. Under the terms of the treaty or *foedus*, the Trevingi Goths were deemed *foederati*, federated troops, and had to provide military support to the Eastern Empire when called upon. It was on that basis that the Goths tolerated the presence of an Eastern Empire Vandal *ala* in the area they controlled. The other large grouping of Goths, the Greuthungi, also became *foederati* and settled further south in Upper Moesia. When Theodosius and his general, Stilico, called for the Goths to join his army, they were obliged to respond.

Now it was Manius with a question. "Master, I can see that Godigsel was in an impossible situation. He had felt it necessary to promise something he could not be sure of delivering. If he failed to deliver Vandal support, then he would make an enemy of Alaric. How did he extricate himself from such a dangerous situation?"

Godigsel had his own plans, and he explained his thinking to us on our return journey but that was only after Alaric had revealed his own grand plan at our farewell meeting.

Chapter 4

Alaric's grand plan

Before we left the Goth camp we had a visit from Alaric and Athaulf. I could see from Godigsel's reaction to Alaric's words that they had discussed the plans beforehand and that this was a repetition for others' benefit. It seemed that both men were already aware of the unrest amongst the tribes living in the Tisza valley. The Vandals, Alans and Samartians living there were coming under increasing pressure from the Goths who lived north of the Danube. Those Goths were themselves under constant pressure from the main body of Huns pushing westwards. Alaric had a clear view of what was to happen.

"Godigsel, on your return you will travel to the Vandal homelands and persuade your father that they should leave those lands and cross the Danube to the north of the Alps. I hear that Raetia is undefended with few Roman troops. The land has been abandoned and will make a fine new homeland for the Vandals. My invasion of Italy will draw Stilico's forces towards me, meaning you will have no real opposition. Any forces the Romans do send north will only weaken the forces I face. I will attack in early summer. Remember that once winter starts the passes across the Alps will be blocked and the Romans will not be able to cross. You will need to convince the Quadi to let you pass through their land. You may well attract some of that tribe to join you. Once you have crossed the Danube send word to me."

Alaric handed Godigsel an ornately decorated scabbard containing a Roman gladius. He drew the sword to show us all a beautifully made weapon with a green jewel embedded in the hilt and explained how he had won the battle trophy.

"I took this from a young Roman tribune at Adrianople. We were both just boys. I was fighting for glory, and he was fighting for his life. He fought well but even this magnificent weapon could not save him. The scabbard and sword are worth a small fortune, and I want you to give it to your father, King Gibamundas, as a gesture of my goodwill. Tell him the time of the Goths and Vandals as enemies is over. We must be allies from now on."

Godigsel made to thank him for his gift, but Alaric wasn't finished explaining his grand plan.

"Asphax, once our campaign starts next month, I want your Alans to be my eyes and ears. Travel ahead of us and send reports of the Roman dispositions. I want you to send your son, Tzason, with Godigsel to the Alan bands living amongst the Vandals. I know you have told me that you have little contact with the Alans in that area, but the presence of your son may just help to persuade them to join with the Vandals in a joint campaign. Send a trusted man to emphasize that young Tzason speaks not only for the Alans of the Sava River but also for Alaric of the Goths."

The thought of Tzason being entrusted with such a mission set our minds racing. I could see Gisselitta quietly resolve to be a part of the mission to Gibamundus whatever Godigsel said. When Alaric turned to his brother-in-law with instructions for our Goth friends then we knew we would definitely be included too.

"Athaulf, I want Indulf and his cousins to also go with Godigsel. Send three of your oathsworn to protect them. They can emphasize that Godigsel's plan is backed by Alaric of the Goths. If any Goth tribes try to interfere with the mobilisation of the Vandals and Alans, then the presence of Athaulf's son may just deter them."

Gisselitta and I exchanged looks. Our trip to the Goth gathering was the biggest adventure of our lives so far. Now it seemed we were going to experience an even bigger one. Godigsel would never have considered taking us on a visit to the Vandal homelands in such troubled times. However, Alaric had demanded that Tzason, Indulf, Traso and Coccas go with Godigsel and there was simply no way we could be excluded.

We left the Goth camp in the last week of March. The Alans and the Goths of our party headed back to the Alan camp and would join us later. We were left to travel back to the summer palace separately and Gisselitta and I took the opportunity to ride on either side of Godigsel. Unusually, he was eager to talk. Godigsel was clearly burdened by the decision he had made. As leader he felt unable to express any uncertainty in front of his men and was glad of the opportunity to explain his choices to his son.

He told us that he had little choice but to go along with Alaric's plans. He would visit the Vandal homelands and consult with his father, King Gibamundas. It seemed to Godigsel that whichever way the Vandals turned, there would be danger. Gisselitta knew to listen when his father spoke but during the silences, he took the opportunity to express his own concerns.

"Father, can we trust Alaric? I am not sure all the Goths will follow him to Italy. Saurus had many supporters. Perhaps Alaric is trying to trick you, and the Vandals, into invading Raetia before he himself invades Italy. If that were to happen, we would face the entire Roman field army and the Goths would have an easy run south of the Alps."

"You are right son. We certainly cannot trust Alaric. Vandals have suffered at the hands of the Goths for centuries. The idea that Alaric needs the Vandals to attack for his plan to succeed is ridiculous. Did you see the number of warriors at the Goth gathering? They must outnumber the Asding Vandals by, at least, twenty to one.

Thousands more live beyond the Danube and threaten our homelands. He will invade regardless of what we do. He will invade whether Saurus backs him or not but when he plans to invade is another question. I too believe he will delay hoping that we will invade first. That is why I will be in no hurry to reach the Vandal homelands. I want to be sure the Goths have invaded before we commit ourselves. Even then I am not sure that your grandfather will be keen on uprooting the people and invading Raetia."

"How will you know what is happening to the south once you cross the Danube?"

"The Alans have been tasked with finding the Roman field army and reporting back to Alaric. My good friend Asphax will send a messenger to the summer palace as soon as the Goth army begins its campaign."

"But what if grandfather and the elders refuse to go along with the plan. Invading Roman territory will have repercussions. I know that the homelands are under increasing Goth and Hun pressure, but surely crossing the Danube and invading Roman territory is a dangerous course to take."

"A dangerous course indeed but to defy Alaric could have disastrous repercussions for us all. He need only send a small warband of Huns or Trivingi Goths and we would have to flee the summer palace.

"What we don't know is the true extent of the unrest in the Tisza valley, and that I must find out. All reports indicate it is gradually getting worse. The Vandals and Alans, even fighting together, would not be able to stop the Danube Goths if they are forced westwards. If the Goths do not come, then it will only be because they have joined the Huns and that combined force would be unstoppable."

Gisselitta seemed to accept all the political considerations quite easily. I, on the other hand, couldn't imagine warriors from our Goth friends camp chasing us out of our home at the summer palace.

Godigsel continued, "If we do move we will need the help of our Quadi neighbours, both in Sirmium and in the Quadi homelands, and our Alemanni friends on the Danube. I will talk to Fredo's father before we leave for the Tisza valley, and we will need Ingamar's father to help us cross the great river."

Our father's main message, however, was that if the Vandals could not be persuaded to invade Raetia as Alaric wanted, then our life at the summer palace would have to end. Although we were technically still Eastern troops the reality was that we had had no pay from Constantinople for years. There would certainly be no support from the Eastern Empire if Alaric decided to attack us. If things did not go according to Alaric's plan the

58

Vandal *ala* would indeed have to move. Godigsel wanted us to be ready for that upheaval.

Gisselitta reflected. "Perhaps we should be like the Alan bands Diomedes told us about in our lessons. Or like Tzason's Sava valley Alans. We should move when we have to move. Even if it means never having a permanent home."

I tried to imagine a life on the move but just could not picture it. The summer palace was all I had ever known. Besides which we were more than just the Vandal troopers. We had a substantial Pannonian community dependent on our presence.

Yannus asked, "Master, I presume the Pannonians were left behind when the great migration began, and all the Alans joined with the Vandals. After all Hunneric is King of the Vandals and the Alans."

The Pannonians in the summer palace community all chose to come with us when we left. Over time they became completely integrated into the Asding Vandals. But as far as the Alans were concerned only some bands came with us.

My answer did not satisfy Yannus.

"Please explain why you refer to some Alan bands. Were they not all one tribe?"

The important thing to remember about the Alans is that they were not just one group or even one people. Separate bands of Alans were everywhere. Two separate bands travelled with us at the start of the great migration. One group under Goar stayed in Gaul and fought for the Romans. The larger group led by Respendial saved our lives when the Franks had us surrounded. It was that group that came with us to Hispania and Africa.

One group stayed with the Goths when Indulf's father, Athaulf, became king after Alaric's death. They eventually settled in Southern Gaul while Goar's people settled near Amorica. At least two groups settled in northern Italy.

Chapter 5

Godigsel's plan

When we arrived back at the summer palace we were in for a surprise. The barracks were alive with activity and extra troops. Gunderic had arrived from the homelands with 100 Vandal warriors. Gunderic was Gisselitta's older half-brother. When we had first met him there was still the element of a youth about him. Now he was a well-built young man of twenty-two or so years with blond hair and beard, the very picture of a Vandal warrior. We sat with Godigsel as Gunderic explained why he had come.

"The situation in the homelands is becoming seriously dangerous. Goth warbands are ranging further and further west. They have fought numerous clashes with the Southern Alans and now increasingly with the Vandals. My men and I caught one small band in the open and destroyed them but the bigger warbands number in the thousands. They may be trying to take the Tisza valley from us and the Alans. Grandfather is worried and he is in poor health. I don't think he has the strength to lead us anymore. He is the only king now that the other co-king, Obadus' father, has died. The elders are demanding that a vigorous young war king be elected to deal with the crisis. Many have called for you, father, to be called back to be war king, but others, particularly the young hot heads of the tribe, favour Obadus."

Godigsel reflected on the news, "Obadus is an experienced warrior. He was with the Roman Vandal *ala* fighting for Eugenious at Fridigus. It was Obadus and his father that Stilico convinced to switch sides that fateful night after the first days' fighting. Apart from that, he is older than me. You know as well as I do that the Vandal tradition is that the oldest relative of the old kings should rule."

Gunderic nodded. "Obadus favours war with the Goths and most of the warriors support him. Gibamundus is fearful that if the Asdings fight alone in a full-scale war it will cost us too many lives. Grandfather has sent me to bring you back."

"And what of the Tisza valley Alans?"

"The Southern Alans are preparing to move and are electing their own war king. Apart from Goth warbands roving through their lands they have Hun raiding parties starting to steal the Alan horse herds and threatening their entire existence. Gibamundus has sent word to them that they are welcome to cross the Tisza and settle with our people on the west bank if necessary. We have not had contact with King Respendial's northern Alans for some time."

Talk of the Alans migrating west brought the conversation round to the expectations that Alaric's Goths had of the Vandals. Gunderic's reaction was that, if Godigsel went back to lead them, most Vandals would follow him. Godigsel's reputation at home was high. However, he had to act quickly, otherwise Obadus would establish himself as war king.

The next morning, we could tell that Godigsel had set his mind on a plan of action and that he intended to act quickly. Fredo was sent with one of our Vandal guards into Sirmium to bring back his father, Vangio, the garrison commander. Gunderic was told he would now command the *ala* for the time being. Godigsel would take 100 of his veteran troops back with him to the Vandal homelands. Gunderic's men would replace them. While we were away Gunderic was to maintain the patrols of the surrounding countryside and thereby keep the local population as calm as possible.

My mother was distressed by all the talk of potentially leaving the summer palace. Godigsel spoke with her privately for a long time before calling me in to join them.

"I have given your mother the option of returning to her kin in Constantinople. I cannot guarantee a secure home for us with all that is happening. You too should have that option of going to the east."

While I took in the full meaning of his words my mother made her position clear. "I will follow your step-father wherever he chooses to go, and I would have both my sons with me."

With that statement any doubt that existed in my mind disappeared.

"I will go wherever Gisselitta goes."

From that point on my mother took on the responsibility of making an evacuation plan for the whole of the summer palace community. It meant organising the construction of wagons, stockpiling food, and finding draught animals and wagon drivers. Gisselitta proposed that the Pannonians in our community should drive the wagons and be given basic military training so that they could act as camp guards.

When Vangio arrived, Godigsel briefed him on the situation and advised the garrison and the people of Sirmium to strengthen their defences, stockpile food but otherwise sit tight until the situation became clearer.

Vangio reported that the tribes in the Quadi homelands were also in a state of agitation and suggested that there would be Quadi warriors eager to join in a raid south of the Danube. He would send a messenger to one of the Quadi tribal chiefs he knew well advising ambassadors to be sent to the Vandals in support of Godigsel's bid to be war king.

Vangio made clear his fears that an all-out attack from the Goths north of the Danube or from Alaric's Goths could not be resisted by his 500 strong cohort, even with a Pannonian militia in support. He added that if he had to abandon the city he felt sure a substantial number of Pannonians would try to come with him.

Godigsel suggested the river route to Aquincum as the safest route home for the Quadi in an emergency. He intended to visit Ingamar's father, the *prefectus* of the Alemanni *ripenses,* on his way to the Vandal homelands and would appraise him of the situation.

Fredo asked his father to let him come with us on the trip. Vangio agreed on condition that one of his Quadi soldiers went with Fredo as a bodyguard.

Godigsel sent urgent messages to the Alan camp for the Alan and Goth contingents to come as soon as possible. While we waited, Godigsel had time to comfort my mother who was upset at the prospect of being temporarily abandoned in the care of Gunderic, a stepson she hardly knew.

She argued that if her sons were going why couldn't she?

Godigsel explained the dangers and the vital responsibility she held to organise and lead the civilian community. Godigsel announced that, if he were successful, he would send us boys back to the summer palace but stay himself with the Vandals and lead them into Raetia. If he did not succeed and

Alaric sought retribution, Gunderic was to abandon the summer palace and bring everyone northwards along the left bank of the river to Aquincum where Godigsel would join them.

Faced with those alternatives my mother came to accept her situation.

On our last night at the summer palace we had time to reflect on our predicament. As a way of distracting us all from the worries and uncertainties we faced, Godigsel encouraged Vangio and Gregor to recall the events which led to the Quadi forming the garrison in Sirmium.

As you will remember it was the absence of a Roman garrison which led to my parents moving out of Sirmium to the summer palace. Gregor had vivid memories of that time.

"When I first arrived in Sirmium in '88 with Marcus' parents, it was a thriving city of artisans and traders fed by the rich farmlands of the surrounding countryside. There must have been about 60,000 people within the walls. The *pretorian prefect*, the one before Marcus' father, presided over a *curia,* or council, of prominent citizens supported by a cohort of Roman soldiers from Illyria. The rampages of the Goths and the Alans throughout Pannonia at that time led to drastic changes to the local environment. The city's population swelled to nearly 100,000 at one point as people abandoned their farms and villages to shelter in the city. Food production dropped and starvation became a regular feature of life in the area. In the city, homelessness, food shortages and endemic crime led to rioting on a regular basis.

"The local garrison, confronted by constant civil disturbances, abandoned their posts as soon as they heard reports of their home villages to the south being threatened. The only aspect of city life that continued as before was the chariot races in the hippodrome. Those with money hired personal guards to protect their families, homes, and businesses. For the general population, the city became a lawless place. We, of course, left to come here where the Vandal *ala* could protect us."

Godigsel continued the story. "I was still a *decurion* in those days and Gibamundus was *prefectus*. A few years later, the great general Stilico visited the summer palace. He was a distant relative of ours and his father had been an Asding Vandal cavalry officer in the Roman army before moving up in the world. As *magister utriusque militae,* he commanded all the troops of the Eastern Empire. Emperor Theodosius and the army of the Eastern Empire was marching west with all the forces they could muster to confront the usurper Eugenius. The key component of the eastern forces was the vast army of Goths led by Alaric.

"Gibamundus' Vandal *ala* was allocated the scouting role on the right flank of the eastern forces with express orders from Stilico to make contact, preferably peaceful contact, with the opposing scouts before the battle. In support Gibamundus had a further squadron of 500 of the local Alans led by Asphax. Stilico anticipated that the opposing cavalry scouts might well be Alan or Vandal troops.

"The Western army had been rapidly put together by taking soldiers away from the Rhine *limes*, the frontier. Franks, Saxons, Alemanni, Marcomanni and Quadi tribesmen all featured in the western forces. The eastern army advanced along the Frigidus River valley through the Julian Alps to be confronted by the western forces blocking their exit. Theodosius threw his Goth troops at the western blockage with disastrous results.

"Thousands of Goths died that day, and the western troops still held their ground. It was in the early evening after the first day's fighting that Gibamundus sent me to Stilico with the message that we had made peaceful contact with opposing *alae* of Vandals and Alans and requesting that Stilico join us north of the mountains.

"In the middle of the night Stilico, with the promise of gold, convinced the western Vandals and Alans to switch sides. It helped that my father knew the leader of the western Vandal *ala* well. We also learnt that the Germanic troops on the Western army's left front were demoralised and did not want to fight again. Armed with this information, Stilico, and our combined force of four *alae*, rode on until we met a Western legion comprising Quadi and Alemanni troops. At this point I should let Vangio tell the story."

Vangio was lost in thought and Fredo had to shake his shoulder before the Quadi *prefectus* could continue.

"I was in command of a cohort of Quadi auxiliaries. In the middle of the night, our scouts brought in Stilico and his entourage. He promised us positions in his army and guaranteed immediate payment of all back pay if our men would stand down when fighting recommenced the next day. Most of us weren't keen to join the Eastern army. We simply did not want to fight for either side. That's when Stilico promised us an easy garrison detail here at Sirmium. When it was agreed, I took Stilico over to the Alemanni cohort next to us. I knew my old friend Hildiger and his men didn't want to fight again either. They wanted to return to their old river frontier positions on the river Rhine.

"So Stilico promised them the best compromise he could think of. They could be *ripenses*, river frontier troops, but on the Upper Danube *limes.* And that, Ingamar, is how your people came to be responsible for the Pannonian *classis.* "

Godigsel concluded the account. "When the battle recommenced, the western army's left flank collapsed. Theodosius had a great victory, and the civil war was over. When Theodosius died the next year, his young sons became emperors, Arcadius in the east, and Honorius in the west. Stilico, married to Theodosius' adopted daughter, Serena, became guardian of Honorius and *de facto* ruler of the Western Roman Empire."

Yannus was confused and wanted me to continue with the main narrative.

"Master, this is interesting detail about the battle of Fridigus, but do we need it for the story of Godigsel's mission to the Vandal homelands?"

You do need to understand all the consequences of that important battle for they are fundamental to all that subsequently happened. The presence of a Quadi garrison at Sirmium and of Alemanni marines at Taurunum were direct consequences of that earlier battle. The Alemanni marines, in particular, played a crucial role in what happened next.

The next morning, we sent Ingamar and Kitan on ahead to Taurunum to warn the Alemanni *prefectus* of our imminent arrival. Over 100 troops would require not only food and accommodation but also transportation, for us and our horses, across the river Danube.

It was the beginning of a time of great disruption for the Vandals, both those at our small community in the summer palace and the thousands in the Vandal homelands across the Danube. The Vandals were not a nomadic people, but Gisselitta had probably been right when he told his father that we should be more like the Alans and move when necessary. The Vandals would be on the move for the next thirty years and we were joined by many other different peoples along the way. The Alans were the most important element of those joining the migration and, but for their intervention, the Asdings would never even have crossed the Rhine.

Before I could continue, Manius intervened with a more nostalgic reminiscence, remembering the last trip we took with Gaeseric to the Alan settlement areas.

"Do you remember, Master, when we last visited Numidia. We followed the Medjerda River down to the great plains and passed one horse farm after another?"

I remembered the trip well. The Alans had settled around the town of Bulla Regis. The area was famous for its horses and had produced the cavalry for Hannibal's campaigns against the Romans. We visited Tzason's son Kossus. We took the trip because Gaeser was Kossus' godfather, and we were concerned for his well-being. Kossus was depressed because he felt that he was losing his leading status in the region as he was then an old man of sixty-five. The old culture of the Alans meant that if you survived to old age and couldn't ride to war or hunt anymore you were dismissed to a low status domestic role. The Alans are Christians now, of course, and thoroughly Romanised and there was no dismissing the immense wealth Kossus had accumulated. Nevertheless, the old beliefs that an Alan warrior should always die in battle still had some influence if only on Kossus himself. Sadly, he died the next year.

Chapter 6

The Alemanni marines and
the Danube fleet

The Alemanni, in their homeland, were Roman *foederati* controlling the Rhine frontier around their main town of Argentorate. They also had responsibility for the Rhine *classis* which patrolled the river all the way north to Mogontiacum. In their new posting they took control of the river patrols on the Danube from the Iron Gates and all the way up the river to Castra Regina, in the land of the Marcomanni. However, the most important stretch of the river was from Singidunum to Aquincum, the stretch which bordered the Vandal homelands.

The Alemanni were the most powerful, and numerous, tribe of the Suebic federation which included the Marcomanni and the Quadi. Of all the Suebic tribes, it was the Alemanni who most favoured the famous Suebic top knot. Every Alemanni man seemed to adopt this distinctive hair style as soon as he came of age whilst only a few of the Quadi wore them. Ingamar had recently started to tie his hair up in this traditional fashion now that he considered himself a man.

From our previous visits to Taurunum we were familiar with the barracks and fortress. The port area could harbour around twenty of the *laburnae*, small river craft, the *ripenses* used. Twenty marines rowed each ship with ten on each side. A single sail could be raised when the wind allowed. The ships had shallow hulls which allowed them to access small tributaries and to run up onto a beach. Aside from the *laburnae*, the *ripenses* also used shallow draft skiffs to transport horses and goods, towing them behind the *liburnae*. The skiffs could also be used for a simple traversing of the river. Back in the days when Rome ruled on both sides of the Danube, army engineers could make a temporary pontoon bridge of the skiffs and ships if a legion army needed to cross the river.

The Eastern Empire still controlled the lower Danube from the *Euxine Sea* as far as the gorge of the Iron Gates. The patrols of the Moesian *classis* ended there. In the period of Goth control of Pannonia, the Pannonian *classis* was free from interference from Constantinople. This meant that, although they received no pay, the *ripenses* were able to profit handsomely from the port duties collected at the busy river ports of Singidunum and Aquincum.

In times of peace, the Danube River was an extremely busy commercial highway. A key tributary, the Tisza River was an important route for traders bringing furs, honey, and amber from the north to the Roman markets. The traditional amber route from the Baltic Sea to Aquileia on the Adriatic Sea passed through both Siling Vandal and Asding Vandal territory. Once the Goths took control of Pannonia, traders found it safer to sell their produce on the Danube in ports such as Aquincum rather than risk the land journey through Pannonia. The *ripenses* patrolled the river to ensure that trading ships could travel unmolested. Of course, they also monitored the border and tried to prevent any illegal crossings. With only a small number of ships to patrol many miles of river, it was impossible to prevent occasional crossings by small numbers of raiders. By the time of our visit, Goth and Hun raids from north of the Danube were becoming increasingly frequent and as a result trade was suffering.

The first evening we arrived, Hildiger, Ingamar's father, took Godigsel and his senior men to a small hall for food and drink while the rest of our travelling party were fed in the barracks. Ingamar was able to persuade his father to let us sit alongside the leaders in the small hall. Hildiger introduced an older man with a weather-beaten face and greying beard as Beremut of the Siling Vandals. Beremut greeted Godigsel in a strangely accented Vandalic.

"My Lord Godigsel, it is an honour to meet you. I am an amber trader from the Siling lands. I have sailed down the Tisza River to bring you urgent messages from Gibamundus. I would have sailed up the Sava to find you, but Hildiger told me he expected you to arrive here shortly."

"Well met, Beremut. What news do you bring from my father?"

"When I docked at the moorings of your father's town of Partiscum several days ago, I was told that Obadus had been elected war king by the Asdings. He was away with a large Vandal warband aiming to confront Goths attacking villages in the north. Gibamundus bade me wait so that I could sail with the latest news and find you. The warband returned claiming success, but with so many missing or dead it seemed to me an expensive victory. The new war king was among the dead. They praised his bravery and said he died well. Your father bids you to come as soon as you can. He suggests you take the river route for there are more than one Goth warband on the loose."

Godigsel was silent while he digested the news. None dared disturb his thoughts. Eventually he turned to Hildiger.

"How long would it take to sail up the Tisza to Partiscum?"

"With a favourable wind and rowing the whole way we could do the journey in two days. By horse it would take you three days."

"Then we go by ship. How many ships do you have available? How many men can you carry? I would leave at dawn tomorrow."

"I have only six ships in port, the rest are on patrol. We could carry all your men but there would be no room for your horses. If we used skiffs to transport the horses it would slow us down so much it would be faster to ride."

"I will take 8 horses for myself and my oathsworn and leave one troop of 30 men here. Would that work?" Hildiger nodded. "I can manage that. I will come and command the fleet myself."

Godigsel clasped arms with the Alemanni *prefectus,* adding his thanks. He then turned to us.

"Gisselitta. You, your friends, and your guards must remain here with the other troopers. It cannot be helped. This journey will be dangerous, and, in any case, we have no room for you. I will send for you as soon as the situation is clear and safe."

Tzason made to speak out, but Godigsel silenced him with a gesture.

"I know, Tzason, that Alaric and your father have tasked you with a mission. We will complete that mission when it is safe to do so. Now, I will not hear any dissent. My decision is made."

When we woke in the morning, we found that the ships had already left. None of us were happy to have been left behind. Tzason was the first to react and it was soon clear he had been planning during the night. Safrax, Tzason's Alan bodyguard, stood before us and explained.

"We will cross the Danube tonight on a skiff with our horses. Ingamar has arranged for men to row us across. We know that there is a large Alan band living only twenty miles from the riverbank.

Ingamar has been there before to buy horses and has volunteered to guide us. We will explain the plans of Asphax and Alaric to their leader and persuade him to ride to Partiscum to help Godigsel."

At this point Indulf joined the discussion. "We Goths will travel with them in case Tzason and Safrax run into any Goths. In this way we will fulfil the roles my father gave us."

I could see that Gisselitta was not to be excluded.

"I will not let my friends travel into danger alone. I will also go, and my Vandal bodyguards will protect us all."

I was not at all convinced that this was the right decision and so I tried to make a case for staying. Godigsel had given strict instructions to remain. I pointed out that the other Vandal troopers would obey that order.

"We will go during the night and simply not tell them," Gisselitta replied.

This was typical of my brother, and I resigned myself to being dragged along with his plans. When we were younger my brother would often lead me into trouble and a beating would result. Now the stakes were much higher, he was putting our lives in danger.

As it happened, the troopers had been making plans of their own. The senior decurion, Guntha, came to us to explain their position. The men were all veterans who had anticipated travelling home to stay. They had families and relatives in the homelands and were worried for their safety. They were deeply frustrated to be left behind by Godigsel. Irrespective of any plans we had been making, or the dangers involved, they had decided to cross the river and ride home. Guntha addressed Gisselitta.

"Young lord. We greatly respect your father's decision, but we cannot see what we achieve by remaining here. We want to go home and protect our families. We believe you will be safe in the fortress with your bodyguards. We wish to cross the river and ride home. The Alemanni have agreed to row us across."

Gisselitta looked around our group one by one and received a nod from each of us in turn. Even Fredo seemed determined to join the adventure. I was not sure it was the right thing to do but I was certainly not going to be the only one to stay.

Gisselitta turned back to Guntha. "We will all go, and we will all go now. Make the preparations."

With hindsight, it was probably a mistake to go in daylight for, I am sure, we were observed from the far bank. As it was, the crossing consumed our every attention. It was a far more difficult process than we had imagined. There was a distinct possibility of a raft capsizing if a horse reared up.

I took reassurance from the fact that I was a strong swimmer thanks to Gregor and Axxa's lessons. As it was, we were lucky that the river was calm, the weather was good, and that we had Safrax with us. Manoeuvring horses onto a skiff takes great patience. Safrax went across several times as he had a certain way with horses which seemed to calm them. Eventually we had all crossed over and were riding hard for the Alan camp.

For an hour we enjoyed the exhilaration of riding in a band of fifty or so warriors. My fears that we would be attacked as soon as we left the riverbank gradually subsided as we followed the bends of the Danube, keeping to the open fields that swept down to the water's edge. To our right the land rose into forested, hilly crags. As we stopped to rest the horses and ourselves, we noticed horsemen in the distance following us.

Suddenly my previous anxieties came flooding back. The Goth guards and Safrax quickly determined that they were Huns.

Guntha tried to take charge. "Vandals form a wedge on me. Once they are within 100 paces, we will charge them," he cried.

I leaned into my brother and reminded him of our lessons. "Remember what Diomedes taught us. The Huns fight like the Alans. They will surround us and riddle us with arrows before there is any chance of contact."

Gisselitta nodded to me and spoke out. "Hold, Guntha. We will lose too many in a charge. We will head for the high ground over there. We ride as far up as we can and then dismount. We youngsters will walk all the horses up into the crags. You warriors will form a shield wall behind us and gradually step back up to the cover of the rocks and trees. We will see just how keen they are on attacking us on foot."

In the last few days Gisselitta's speech had become increasingly croaky as his voice was breaking. Now, for the first time, we heard an almost adult voice. I am sure Guntha wanted to dispute the instruction but there was no time to argue. Guntha barked, "Do as Gisselitta commands."

We rode hard for the high ground. We sat there for two hours amongst the trees and crags staring down at the band of fifty or so Huns milling around at the base of the rocky slope. The Huns had a reputation of never dismounting to fight and I prayed that it would be true in this case. One Hun tried a long shot with his bow, but we were 400 metres up and clearly out of range. The Huns remained on their horses the whole time and eventually turned away and left.

We waited another hour and then Safrax volunteered to go down to scout the area. Once he returned and gave the all-clear we all went down and resumed our journey. We were nervous for the rest of the day but by dusk we had acquired Alan outriders who guided us into their camp.

I could see that Yannus was still confused by the reference to different bands of Alans. He asked, "Why did the Alans splinter into so many different bands when together they could have been a much more powerful force?"

The Huns burst out of the East in the 370s, and it was the Alans more than any other group who were the first to suffer. The Alans fought numerous battles with the Huns but found them to be both more ferocious and more numerous. The Huns rode similar steppe ponies and were equally skilled horsemen. Their battle tactics differed little from Alanic fighting tactics. It was the use of the recurve bow from horseback that distinguished the Huns from others. A Hun warrior trained with a bow from an early age. With strong arms, the bow could be drawn to a much greater extent than other bows resulting in a range of almost 300 metres. Most Alan warriors relied on throwing javelins with only a few horse archers in support. Every Hun warrior was a horse archer, and they could devastate an enemy army even before close combat had commenced. Over time, the Huns subdued the Alans. The different Alan bands had a simple choice. Join with the Huns, fight for them and accept Hun overlordship or flee to the West. Many of the Alan bands fled West to join with the Goths who were the next in line to suffer constant Hun raids.

The Goths suffered in a similar fashion to the Alans before them until, in desperation, they begged the Eastern Empire to allow them to cross the Danube. The Romans did let them cross, but then treated the refugee peoples so badly that armed revolt was the only choice. The Battle of Adrianople, which we have already mentioned, was the result.

Yannus was still not satisfied. "I can see that the Alans who lived along the Sava River near to you originated from the mixed band of Goths and others who crossed the Danube in 376 but what I don't understand is how the Vandal homelands along the Tisza had been mixing with Alan peoples for hundreds of years before this."

Whilst the Huns drove thousands of Alans and Goths westward in the 370s, many other Alan bands had raided and then settled in the West over the previous 300 years. The grazing lands of the Tisza valley were particularly attractive to a nomadic people with large herds of horses and other animals. The Iazyges had settled there, before the Alans and the Vandals arrived, for the very same reasons. During the long Marcomannic wars in the second century, the Asding Vandals had been brought south from beyond the Tatra mountains by the Romans to fight as mercenary allies against the Marcomanni, the Quadi, the Samartian Iazyges and, no doubt, some Alan bands. After the Emperor Marcus Aurelias had eventually won the war, some 8,000 Samartians and Alans were conscripted into the Roman army as cavalry. Some of the newly formed *alae* were sent to Britannia and, indeed, at least one Vandal *ala* was sent there with them. It was quite a shock when Gaeser and I came across a Briton Vandal *ala* in Gaul in 407. They were descendants of an old Vandal *ala* sent to Britannia hundreds of years before. The usurper Constantine had brought them across with the Roman legions from Britannia in his attempt to take over the Empire and we ran right into them.

Manius gently prompted me to move on. "With respect may I suggest, Master, that we leave that account to its appropriate place in the story."

Chapter 7

The Vandal and Alan homelands

The Alan camp was a vastly different affair to Tzason's camp on the Sava River. It was clearly an established settlement with permanent wooden buildings scattered throughout the camp. Covered wagons provided the accommodation for those without a wooden lodge. We were taken to the largest wooden structure which seemed to serve as a place of assembly. With Safrax and Tzason in the fore, we were taken to meet the leader of the band. The Alan leader and Safrax spoke in Alanic for some time with occasional contributions from Tzason. Finally, the leader turned to us and introduced himself in Vandalic.

"I am Goar, of the southern Alan and Iazyges bands of the Tisza valley. I understand we have here the son of Godigsel of our friends the Asdings."

My brother stepped forward. "I am Gisselitta of the Asdings. May I present Indulf, son of Athaulf of the Tervingi Goths and his two cousins. This is Fredobodus, son of Vangio of the Quadi, prefectus at Sirmium and this is …"

"I know this young man, who I see now sports a top knot. Welcome back Ingamar. How is your father, Hildiger?"

"He is well Lord. He has taken Godigsel and his troops to Partiscum. He should have arrived by tomorrow."

"It is well that he has gone. The Asdings fought against a large Goth warband a couple of weeks ago and did not fare well. I hear they lost their king. I don't know what the Goths will do next. We will travel with you to Partiscum and support the Asdings in case there is need."

During the evening we learnt much about Goar's people. The community around us were working hard on the construction of more wagons. We saw one wooden lodge being dismantled to provide timber. The tribe was preparing to move but not the seasonal move the Sava River Alans routinely made. Goar was a young man and had only recently been chosen as leader. He confirmed that his people were making ready to move if they had to. They were suffering from repeated raids from small bands of Huns. We told him of our own encounter with Huns and he was surprised only by the fact that we escaped them. Goar was a vigorous and energetic man and he had been chosen to lead the community to new lands. They had been in the area for hundreds of years, and the Samartian Iazyges before them for even longer. The wooden buildings were built by the Iazyges long ago and since then Alans and Iazyges had merged into one people.

In the morning we awoke to find over 100 Alan warriors assembled and ready to ride. We stared in amazement at the sight of twelve female warriors amongst them. Goar was amused at our astonishment.

"The Iazygi have a tradition of young female warriors fighting alongside the men. It has been a part of their culture for centuries."

I reminded Gisselitta about the time Diomedes had read to us from Herodotus about the Amazons. Perhaps the Amazons had been Samartian Iazygi.

Each warrior led a second horse and, in order not to slow down the warband, we were each lent a spare horse. We had 150 miles to cover and, with the spare horses, Goar explained that we should get there in two days. If the previous day's ride from the river had been exciting, then it paled in comparison to riding with the Alans. Nevertheless, I was extremely nervous given the events of the previous day. As if reading my mind, Goar rode up and spoke to me.

"Do not look so fearful young man. The Hun raiders rarely number more than 50. They would never attempt to attack us."

On the first day we passed two other Alan camps where more warriors joined us. By the start of the second day, we numbered over 300. We came across the first Vandal villages on that second morning. The first had been recently abandoned and must have suffered an attack by Huns or Goths.

A warrior brought Goar an arrow and he confirmed that it had been a Hun attack. The next Vandal village was fortified with wagons in between the Vandal longhouses, herds of animals crammed inside the perimeter and warriors guarding the barriers. There were relieved waves from the village when they recognised that we were Alans and no danger to them.

In the afternoon Alan scouts came riding in to report to Goar the approach of a small band of riders. At first, we thought this was another band of Alans come to join us. Safrax confirmed that they were Alans, but they would not approach any closer to us than 400 metres. They simply waited. Goar and two of his senior men rode out to talk to them. After lengthy discussions, the new band rode away taking one of Goar's men with them. One warrior from the new Alan band returned with Goar. At the evening meal we all listened carefully as Goar explained:

"We are close to Partiscum now. Those riders were from the northern Alan bands who are led by Respendial. They are 200 strong and are camped a few miles to the north of us. They say that there is a huge Goth warband camped on a small hill a mile outside of Partiscum. The Vandals are trapped in the town. Between the hill and the town is flat open ground ideal for Alan horses. The Goths are on foot but there are at least 2,000 of them. Respendial's man here, tells us they have seen ships arrive in the town today with warriors on board."

"That will be my father and his men," Gisselitta blurted out.

"Respendial's camp is to the north of the plain and he believes the Goths are unaware of his presence. He is reluctant to attack against so many but, now that we are here, he may change his mind. We don't know how many Vandal warriors they have in the town. Maybe, if we coordinate our attack, we can defeat the Goths."

"My father has 70 veterans from the *ala*, but most don't have horses", Gisselitta contributed.

"If the ships are still there, then there will be 120 Alemanni marines with my father", Ingamar added.

"I doubt there are as many as 500 fighting men from the town. The numbers are still against us," said Goar considering the options.

"Maybe we don't have to fight them. They may not be Trevingi, but they are still Goths. I will go and speak to them," announced Indulf. "We will approach with a branch of peace. They will respect the name of Athaulf. My father sent us here for this purpose. We will persuade them to leave peacefully."

Goar expressed his concerns. "You can try but I doubt they will leave. Whatever you do, do not reveal our presence here or Respendial's men close by. We must retain surprise on our side and, if we can, get word to the town."

"Let me go with Indulf and I will see if they let me through to the town," Gisselitta put forward.

Axxa would have none of it. "I will not allow you to go."

My brother was undeterred. "Listen to me. With our two hidden cavalry wings and the forces in the town, I believe we have here the possibility to recreate the Battle of Cannae from the Punic wars, when Hannibal defeated the Romans."

I was embarrassed by my brother's audacity and wished he had kept quiet. I felt sure the adults would mock him. While we boys had all studied the battle together and had a vague understanding of what Gisselitta meant, the adults had no idea and just looked bemused. Nevertheless, they allowed Gisselitta to explain his plan in more detail.

"If I get through to the town tomorrow, I will ask my father to advance his forces out onto the plain in front of the town barriers. He will advance a short distance and then stop and form a shield wall. This should entice the Goth hoard to come down off the hill and attack across the plain. With their overwhelming numbers the Goths will be unable to resist the opportunity. When the Goths are charging across the plain they will be vulnerable to a flank attack. That will be the time for Respendial's men to attack from the north and your men, lord, to attack from the south. The Vandals will retreat to the barriers dragging the Goths further on. The Vandals will be the bull's head and you, Lord Goar, will be one of the bull's horns and Respendial's men will be the other. You must try to encircle them so that the two bull's horns meet behind the Goths. For Hannibal, his Numidian cavalry were his bull's horns; for us it will be the Alan horsemen of the Tisza valley."

I could not believe the confidence with which my brother had delivered his battle plan. Diomedes would have been proud of his pupil's knowledge of the famous battle. We turned to see what Goar would make of a twelve-year-old's plan.

"I know not this Hannibal you speak of, but I do know the Goths will not withstand an Alan ambush from both flanks at the same time. We have a plan. Let's make it happen."

With that Goar sent Respendial's man back to his leader with the battle plan for the next day.

"Master, you must have felt compelled to go with Gaeseric, I mean Gisselitta. How did you feel knowing that you had to face a Goth warband the next day?" asked Yannus.

I was not the only one who felt compelled to go with Gisselitta. If Indulf and my brother were going then we were all going. I was physically sick with worry and could not sleep at all. When we rode out in the morning, I looked at the others and saw their determination to look confident even though I knew they were not. I steeled myself to do the same.

We considered that the presence of 30 Vandal troopers from the *ala* would be too provocative and so they had left with the Alans. Axxa and our bodyguards were another matter, and they would not leave us under any circumstance. Our party of eight boys and eleven guards rode slowly to the Goth camp at dawn. The Alan warband were nowhere to be seen. Indulf was in the front with Traso and Coccas either side of him. The twins both carried leafy branches above their heads. Indulf assured us the Goths would honour the symbol of peaceful intent they signified. I was not convinced and spoke my concerns to my brother.

"Our guards will be a provocation to the Goths. You know as well as I, that if the Goth warriors feel challenged in any way they will simply attack us."

Gisselitta agreed and spoke to Indulf. As we closed to within 100 metres of the camp our guards stopped and let us ride on alone. Even at a distance it was clear that we were a group of youths and that we posed no threat. There was no honour to be had in attacking a group of boys.

"Who in the name of the gods are you," barked the first Goth sentry.

"I am Indulf, son of Athaulf of the Trevingi Goths. Who leads here?" announced Indulf trying to sound important.

One of the guards left and, after a short delay, a giant of a man strode up. He wore a gold torc and multiple golden arm bands and carried a huge axe. A dozen of his heavily armed oathsworn warriors stood behind him.

"I am Radagarius, leader of all the Goths north of the river," he bellowed. "Are you lost Trevingi striplings?"

"Break off your attack on the Vandal town. Those people are under the protection of Alaric, the king of the Goths, south of the river. We need their warriors in our campaign against the Romans," Indulf declared boldly.

"So you claim to be Athaulf's boy. I have heard of him, and I know the reputation of Alaric. You all follow the white Christ and serve the Romans. I care not what Alaric and his Christian God want. I certainly will not take orders from the spawn of his tribe. You three may be Goths, but those boys behind you look like Suebes to me judging by the top knot that one has. And if I am not mistaken that is a mongrel Alan and the other a mere slave. Ride away now, and take those warriors over there with you, while I am in a good mood. I am busy. I have some Vandals to kill."

Gisselitta edged his horse forward. "I am Gisselitta of the Asding Vandals whose town you are attacking. My father, Godigsel, commands over there and he has his veteran elite troops from the Roman army with him along with Alemanni marines from the Roman river fleet and the Vandal warriors of the town. A Quadi army marches to support us and will be here soon. If you attack the town this day you may win the battle, but you will lose a great many of your men. Men you cannot afford to lose with the Huns coming from the east in ever greater numbers."

Gisselitta's words clearly had an effect. Radagarius was silent for a while before replying.

"Wise words young Vandal. It is true I do not wish to lose men here today. I would rather have your Vandals join us. The Huns are coming for you as much as for us. If we were to combine our forces, then, maybe, we could hold them off. If not, we will be strong enough to force a crossing of the river and take new land. Your father needs to surrender the town if he wants to protect his womenfolk and children. You have my word there will be no killing, pillaging, or raping. All his men are welcome to join us under my command. What say you? Will you take this message to your father?"

"I will take your message. But if I go, my friends go with me, and our guards come too."

"So be it. We will wait until the midday sun. If we do not hear back by then, we attack, and all will perish including you. I want this done quickly!"

Gisselitta signalled the guards to join us. Radagarius' voice boomed out a command for us to be let through and with a wave of his hand the Goth hoard that had gathered around us parted, leaving a path to the town. Slowly we urged our horses through the gap. It was noticeable that, while those around Radagarius appeared as fearsome and well-armed warriors, the rest of the Goth band were younger warriors with only a spear and shield. It was these younger looking warriors who called out insults and made gestures as we passed through their ranks though none dared to obstruct us. We cantered across the plain, now with Gisselitta in front and Ingamar and me, on each side, carrying the peace branches just in case we were not recognised.

Manius queried the reference to Radagarius.

"Master, I am aware of a Goth leader called Radagarius. He is said to have led 200,000 Goths into Italy in 406. Why did he have only a small warband when you encountered him?"

Although he claimed to be the leader of the Goths north of the Danube when we met him, I don't think he was any more than one warband leader out of many at that time. Part of the reason why the Huns were able to conquer the Goths was because the Goths were not unified. There was no overall leader to rally the various Goth tribes. Only when different groups had fought against the Huns and lost, did the survivors start to consolidate around Radagarius, their most successful warband leader.

Chapter 8

My first battle

It was mid-April when we slowly rode towards the barriers blocking the track leading into the town. Godigsel and Hildiger stood together on an upturned wagon staring incredulously at our approach. A gap was created to allow us access to the town. Vandal longhouses lined the main street, each with its own area of land behind. Partiscum had once been a Roman fort and I could distinguish the grid pattern of the town's streets. The outer town appeared to me as a complete jumble of houses and lanes. If this was the Vandal capital I was not impressed. We were guided to a stone building in the centre which served as the residence for the ruling kings. Gibamundus greeted us warmly while there was a rougher welcome for Gisselitta from Godigsel. Hildiger cuffed Ingamar around the ears before hugging his son close. I could see that Godigsel wanted to take Axxa to task for exposing us to such danger but all explanations as to how we had come to be there had to wait. There was only one thing on everyone's minds. When would the Goths begin their attack on the town?

Gisselitta spoke privately with his father repeating the terms of Radagarius' offer. Then

Godigsel turned and announced that we had two hours to organise our battle plans. The Goths would attack at midday unless we surrendered. We were surprised to hear that some of the town elders who gathered around us were in favour of surrendering and joining with the Goths. A lot of the families who had lost sons and fathers at the recent battle were resigned to the Goths taking over the town. Only 400 of the town's warriors had returned from Obadus' so-called victory. There were many more men in the town, but they were the craftsmen, traders, and labourers of the settlement. Gibamundus admonished them and said they should have faith in his son. It was the signal for Godigsel to take charge.

"Elders leave us. My son, Gisselitta, has told me how we can win this battle and I have faith in his plan. We must prepare."

Godigsel turned to Hildiger. "This is not your battle my friend. Take your men and your ships and leave. None will judge you for it."

Hildiger replied, "We will stand with our Vandal friends come what may. If we fare badly, we can fight our way back to our ships and some might survive."

Godigsel thanked him for his support and called for the Vandal warriors of the town, the Vandal troopers and the Alemanni *ripenses* to gather round.

"There will be no surrender here today and no retreat to the river. We have Alan allies waiting to join the battle. With their surprise attack on the flanks, we can not only hold the Goths but beat them. Gisselitta, go through the battle plan again so that we may all be clear."

Gisselitta spoke with authority and clarity. "At noon, the Vandal troopers and the Alemanni marines should form line in front of the barriers. The Vandal warriors of the town should remain on the barricades supported by the townsfolk willing to fight. With our own bodyguards joining we can make a line of 200 experienced and well-armed troops. The line will advance 100 metres towards the Goths. We want to show the Goths how few we are compared to them. When they see our numbers, they will charge us for they can easily outflank us on both sides. This is important for we want to entice the Goths down off their hill and onto the plain.

"The Alan warriors of Goar and Respendial are waiting for the moment when the Goths are exposed on the open plain. Once the Goths charge, and I promise you they will, the line should retreat once more back to the barrier. The Goths will think we are afraid of them. That is what we want. We want to bring the Goths further forward so that they are defenceless against the Alan cavalry attacks from both sides.

"Our retreat must be step-by-step, all together with absolute discipline. The barriers are our last line. There can be no retreat from there. The troopers and marines will hold the shield wall line in front of the barriers with the warriors of the town on the barriers holding spears over their heads. Arrows and sling shots can be fired over the wall by youngsters and those women willing to fight. We will be the bull's head and the Alans will be the bull's horns. The Alans will try to completely encircle the Goths. We can win this battle if we follow the plan."

Godigsel looked at Gisselitta with a new respect and took charge once more.

"I will be the centre of the line with my oathsworn. The Vandal troopers will be to my right. The bodyguards can join the line at the far right. Hildiger your marines will take the left side. We march forward on my step, and we retreat on my step. Do not break the line under any circumstance.

"Gibamundus, you will command the Vandal warriors on the barricades with the townsfolk, the youths, and the women willing to fight. Have the younger boys ready with water bottles behind the barrier. Now go and prepare yourselves. In one hour, we advance on the enemy."

Our gang of eight came together to decide how we would face our first battle. This was a long way from the mock battles with wooden swords at the summer palace. We each carried short swords and small shields, but they seemed puny weapons compared to those of the troopers. All the troopers carried spears and, whilst the marines didn't, they soon acquired some from the townsfolk. We decided we too needed long spears. There was a plentiful supply, and we were soon suitably armed. Fredo declared that he was going to join the front line and marched off to find his bodyguard. Indulf then left to find his Goth guards on a similar mission. Both returned shortly making a show of their disappointment. The bodyguards would not risk their charges in the front line. As a compromise the guards had said that Fredo, Indulf, Traso and Coccas could stand on the barrier behind the position of the guards. Safrax would not allow Tzason to join them. Instead, he handed Tzason his bow and quiver and told him to climb up onto the top of the nearest longhouse. Gisselitta, Ingamar and I had already decided we would stand with Gibamundus on the middle barrier directly behind Godigsel and Hildiger. Once all was decided we formed a circle, placed our hands together and pledged our allegiance to each other. We nervously broke apart with hugs, slapped backs and not a little bravado, to take up our positions. Once next to Gibamundus I could not disguise the fear I felt, and the old man could see it in my eyes. He spoke words to comfort me since it was apparent that Gisselitta needed none.

"Be strong Marcus. Remember your weapons training and watch your brother's back. Make sure he doesn't do anything reckless!"

As the sun approached its highest point, the troopers, marines, and guards stepped out from the barrier. They formed line with oval shield next to oval shield and spears held upright.

"One hundred paces advance," roared Godigsel.

The soldiers tramped forward in silence. After 50 metres we noticed activity far away on the hill where the Goths awaited. A small group of six Goth riders broke out of the mass and galloped towards the line. Well out of bow shot range, they rode from one end of the line to the other and then turned back to the hill. At one hundred paces the line halted. For what seemed the longest period nothing happened. Godigsel advanced the line ten steps further forward. I could hear Gisselitta speak his thoughts aloud urging our father not to go too far. At last, a response but, not quite, what we were expecting. A huge body of Goths began to walk towards us. There was easily enough to overwhelm the line. The problem was that plenty more Goths remained on the hill with Radagarius, and his mounted oathsworn warriors.

I was the one to mouth the fears we all thought.

"What will Goar and Respendial do if the Goths split into two? If they attack the first group, they will leave themselves open to counterattack from the second group."

It was Gibamundus who calmed our nerves.

"I have fought with Alans before. You mark my words. They will not be caught in close contact fighting. If the Goths can withstand the hail of javelins from the Alans, then we will have an almighty fight on our hands. But I somehow think that the Goths are not committed to an all-out battle and that's why they haven't committed all their men. They want to cow us Vandals into joining forces with them. They do not want to lose any more men."

As the Goths closed with the Vandal formation, we could hear Godigsel give the command to step back. As the line retreated, the Goths began to jog forwards and rapidly narrowed the gap.

Gisselitta spoke his thoughts aloud, "Now would be a good time, pray God they come now."

Tzason shouted from the roof top. "I see Goar's Alans."

A hundred Alan warriors were galloping towards the flank of the Goths. The Vandal line was now just ten metres from the barriers. Arrows and stones flew from the wagon barricade, over the heads of the Vandal line, to strike the Goths. Tzason was releasing arrow after arrow. I was thankful that very few missiles came back the other way. I held my shield tight to my body and made sure Gisselitta was doing the same. My body was ready to act but there was, in fact, nothing to be done. We held our position on the wagon and I

103

prayed that Godigsel and Hildiger's men would protect us from the onslaught.

The shield wall of the troopers and marines was bristling with spears and was a formidable obstacle to attack. Nevertheless Goth warriors threw themselves at the defenders using axes to drag down the shields. The shield wall buckled under the pressure of so many Goths pushing against it. Before they could break through, a hail of javelins suddenly hit the Goth advance from the side. As the Alan horses turned away in perfect unison, the next wave was there with another volley. The Alans were attacking in three waves of 100 warriors. The cycle of attacks was continuous. The main body of Goths stopped moving forward and turned right to shield themselves from the Alan javelins.

In that moment I realised that Radagarius had sent his younger warriors to attack us. There was an air of desperation amongst them as, almost unnoticed, the Alans of Respendial appeared on the left behind them and launched their own volley of javelins. Again, it was wave after wave of javelin volleys. Behind the Goths, thirty mounted Vandal troopers led by Guntha made their own attack. Godigsel, sensing the opportunity, cried out for the line to advance on his step. Only a handful of Goths remained to fight, a substantial number were dead or wounded but the majority were running back to the hill trying to evade the Vandal troopers. The

Alans and Vandals together delighted in chasing them down. A fleeing man is an easy target.

I know not the exact numbers, but it was said that six hundred Goths died that day. Of course, the battle was not necessarily over. Radagarius remained on the hill with a large body of warriors around him. The Alan warriors and Guntha's troopers joined together on the plain to face the hill. The Goths still outnumbered the assembled allied forces, but Radagarius could see that, without cavalry, he could not prevail. Radagarius and his oathsworn turned their horses away and the Goth warriors trudged after them. The Battle of Partiscum was over.

I would fight in many battles during the great migration and, as battles go, this was a gentle introduction. The fear that possessed my every sinew disappeared when the fighting began. I took great comfort in standing beside Gibamundus. I was ready to act even though there was nothing I had to do. If the old man had said charge, I would have charged. If he had said run, I would have run.

Now it was Yannus with the question.

"Master why were there so few warriors in the town. There were many thousands on the great migration. Why weren't there more warriors at the battle?"

The Asding Vandals were country dwellers spread out across the Vandal homelands on both sides of the Tisza River. Partiscum was the only Vandal town, and it was small compared to Sirmium. The Goth warband had taken the town by surprise just after many of the town's warriors had perished with Obadus in the previous battle. There was no time to call for reinforcements from the surrounding villages. It was fortunate that Godigsel and Hildiger had arrived when they did.

Chapter 9

The aftermath of the battle

After it became clear that the hostilities were over, we were euphoric. Our gang joined together once again, and each related their own personal experience. Women went around the warriors with buckets of beer and water. We helped ourselves to our share of beer. Most of the warriors had collapsed on the ground where they had stood. Gibamundus explained that this was normal behaviour after a battle. There was no greater exertion than fighting for your life. We pointed to the field where swarms of Alans were stripping the dead of weapons, armour, coins, and anything of value even clothes.

"That too is normal," Gibamundus continued, "to the winner the spoils. We will let the Alans take the plunder. I think they deserve it. Your father and I took massive amounts of treasure after the battle of Frigidus."

Our guards joined us after they had rested awhile. Axxa was proud of how his men had performed and we had new respect for them. Our relationship with them changed that day. Axxa was older and more experienced but Kitan, Otte, Skara, Ulli and Wada were little older than us and it had been their first battle. We had been involved but we had not been on the front line like they had. We praised their courage and we hoped we would perform as bravely when our turn came.

For the first time we became aware of our guards as important members of Vandal families. Both Wada and Otte had families from Partiscum. Otte was dragged away by his parents and siblings in a joyous reunion. Wada's mother pulled him away from the others to tell of his father's death fighting with Obadus. Regardless of Wada's sadness, the celebrations continued.

Tzason recounted how he shot an arrow into the chest of a Goth. Our friend then demonstrated, for comic effect, how the warrior had simply snapped the arrow off and thrown it away. We all laughed. Skara showed us his shield which had a large piece missing at the top. He explained that a Goth axe had hacked into the shield and pulled it down leaving him defenceless. Axxa had saved him by pushing his own shield in front of Skara just as a spear was coming to end his life. Axxa took the opportunity to repeat the training ground lesson we had heard so many times before.

"Your shield protects you and your left side partner's sword side. Your right-hand partner protects himself and your sword side. You must always fight together as one."

The Goth guards and Fredo's guard were more experienced fighters, but they nevertheless tolerated Axxa's instructions and our general excitement.

By the evening everything had started to settle down. The Vandals were all back in town. Drunken parties spilled out of every longhouse and there was raucous singing in the streets. Vandal warriors and townswomen were openly coupling in the long grass. The Alemanni marines had repaired to their ships with wine skins, food, and any local women willing to join them. Ingamar was tracked by a group of young girls of our age and eventually left us to go with them. He pulled Fredo along with him.

Tzason left us to go out to the vast Alan camp which now dominated the plain. He and Safrax said they wanted to find Respendial and thank him personally for his intervention. We had all seen Goar after the battle when he came and clasped hands with Godigsel. Both men made a point of praising Gisselitta for his battle plan and his bravery in riding into the Goth camp to confront Radagarius. Gisselitta generously deflected the praise to Indulf as it was his idea that we should approach the Goths.

Despite this we could see that Indulf, Traso and Coccas felt a little left out. The town people recognised them as Goths and failed to distinguish them from those that had attacked the town. Eventually, as it became dark, we settled around a campfire with Gibamundus and enjoyed roasted goat and more beer than we could handle as we listened to one battle anecdote after another.

Godigsel and Hildiger were absent dealing with wounded troopers and marines of whom there were several. Arrangements had to be made for the one Vandal trooper who had died of his wounds. Godigsel felt it was important for the man to have a proper Christian burial which was a novelty for the mostly pagan townsfolk. The disposal of hundreds of dead bodies on the plane was also a priority for him. He said they had to be burnt before disease spread to the Alan camp and the town. He collected parties of volunteers who gathered the bodies into a huge pile in between the two Alan camps. With wood piled on top the pyre blazed all night, giving off a pungent smell all through the following days.

The next day began slowly. By midday Gibamundus had collected the town elders together in front of his stone residence and asked them to confirm Godigsel as war king of the Vandals. There had been no time before the battle. The warriors and towns folk gathered around to voice their support. So, by popular acclaim Godigsel was elected the Vandal war king.

Gibamundas presented Godigsel with the scabbard and sword Alaric had gifted to the King of the Vandals.

"You are the king now, son. You should have this sword."

Hildiger was the first to congratulate him. Respendial and his senior men rode in with Safrax and Tzason and received the cheers of everyone there. Goar and his men had been in the town most of the day mixing freely with the people. With the leaders of the different groups all present, Godigsel declared a meeting that evening to discuss the situation they all faced. The problem was not only the prospect of renewed attacks from the North Danube Goths and the Huns but the demands of Alaric, King of the Southern Goths.

At the meeting that evening Godigsel made a point of having Gisselitta by his side as he spoke at length with each of the leaders in turn. I was beside my brother as we heard the plans and fears of each group. Godigsel briefed each leader on the threats we faced, the opportunities an invasion of Raetia presented and the consequences of doing nothing. He also listened carefully to their responses and, when he felt all had been said, he called on each leader to state their intentions.

Goar was the first to speak. I believe he made his decision some time before.

"The Southern Alan and Iazygi bands that I lead will leave the Tisza valley. We will migrate to Raetia as Godigsel suggests. If we must, we will fight for land, but I hope we can come to a peaceful arrangement with the Romans. I will bring my people here to cross the Tisza and would ask for help to cross the river. We will ask the Quadi for

111

permission to cross their land and travel north of the Danube until we get to the river Enns. We will cross into Raetia there before we enter Marcomanni territory. We would welcome the company of the Asdings and the Northern Alans."

Respendial duly spoke next.

"We thank our brother Goar for his invitation. We Alans in the north have not been troubled overly by the Hun raids. As for the Goths, we have many more warriors than the southern Alans and we believe we can resist them. We will not give up the grazing lands that have supported our communities and our horse and animal herds for so long. The northern Alans will remain for the time being. If the Huns come against us in strength, then that is the time we will move west."

Godigsel spoke for the Vandals. I could see that Gibamundus was in full agreement with his son's words.

"I will lead a war party of Vandals to Raetia. We will accompany the Southern Alans. We will explore whether the province is the right place for all the Asding Vandals to move to at a future point. My father will remain here and lead the people in building a defensive wall around Partiscum. We will send messengers to every Vandal village advising them to build their own defences or, if they cannot, to move to the nearest defensible village or to come here. We will ask for volunteers to assemble here if they wish to join my war party.

The volunteers will help build rafts for the crossing of the Tisza so that we can carry the Alan wagons, all our horses and ourselves across the river.

"Within the next few days, I expect an embassy from the Quadi to arrive here. I am sure they will not only allow us to travel across their territory but also join us in crossing into Raetia. I propose that we leave in one month's time. Is that sufficient time for your people to get here, Goar?"

"It is enough time. We have been preparing for the last few months. To thank you for your help with the crossing we will give you horses so that all your warriors will be mounted once more. I do not want to see you fighting on foot again," Goar joked.

Godigsel thanked Goar for the offer of new mounts and nodded to Hildiger. "Hildiger, in gratitude for your support yesterday, you may keep the horses we left at Taurunum. They may be useful in an emergency."

Hildiger spoke.

"I and the Alemanni marines will return to Taurunum. Whilst there is commercial traffic on the river we will remain there. We have our fortress, and we have our ships. We will be safe. I will stop our patrols up the river at the fortress of Lauriacum on the Enns tributary. That way we shall be blind to your crossing. You should pass by the fortress but cross before you reach Lentia.

There used to be a Roman *ala* based there. I am not sure if it still is."

In the next few days things started to happen. Kitan, Skara and Ulli asked for leave so that they could be the messengers to their own villages and have an opportunity to visit their families. Axxa gave his permission once Otte and Wada had been released by their families. One morning the tent city of Respendial's Alans disappeared. We would not see them again for several years.

Goar's warriors left to escort their people to Partiscum. Hildiger's ships left taking our friends Ingamar, Indulf, Traso, Coccus, Tzason and their guards with them. It was a sad parting as we had experienced much together. The Goth boys were keen to find Alaric and report that the Vandals and Alans were on the move.

I had fully expected to be returning with the others as Godigsel had promised our mother that he would send Gisselitta and me back to the summer palace if the invasion of Raetia were to go ahead. He now broke that promise stating that he wanted Gisselitta with him on the campaign. He also wanted Fredo to remain so that he could help with communications as we passed through Quadi lands. His value was immediately apparent as, the day after our friends left, five Quadi warriors appeared across the other side of the river. Fredo was delighted to find out that their leader, Marobus, was a distant relative of his father,

114

Vangio. Fredo attended all the meetings between the Quadi leader and Godigsel. Marobus made it clear that the Quadi were eager to join the venture to Raetia. He claimed hundreds of Quadi warriors would join the convoy as they progressed across Quadi land to the river. Marobus promised to lead them himself.

All through the next few days small groups of Vandal warriors arrived in response to the messengers Godigsel had sent out to the villages. Kitan, Skara and Ulli all returned with small groups of their friends from their home villages. The Vandal youngsters wanted to join Godigsel's warband. Gibamundus set them to work building rafts for the river crossing. The first convoy to arrive at the town was not the one we expected. A wagon train of over fifty vehicles crawled across the plain escorted by around thirty mounted warriors and twice that number of warriors on foot. Gibamundus knew who there were. He said that they called themselves the Lacringi Vandals although Gibamundus was not sure they were Vandals at all.

Their leader, Crixos, greeted Godigsel in a Goth accented Vandalic. Gibamundus explained that the Lacringi had been living to the north of the Vandal lands for some months. Crixos told the story of what had brought them west. They had lived far to the east where the Heruli and the Gepids lived. The Huns had invaded their territory and defeated them. Most of the tribe had bent the knee to the new Hun leader, Uldin, and now fought for him. The Heruli and the Gepids had also succumbed to Hun rule. The Lacringi before us now had lived in a remote valley and had managed to escape to the Vandal lands last Autumn. When they heard that Godigsel and the Alans were planning to invade Raetia they all decided to join the migration. They feared that sooner or later the Huns would catch up with them. Godigsel accepted them with open arms and Gibamundus set the men to work making rafts.

The arrival of the Southern Alans and Iazygi was a different matter. The whole plain gradually filled with what seemed like a thousand wagons. Within a day a massive Alan city of wagons and tents had been established. It was easily bigger than the town. Godigsel had amassed a war party of 1,000 warriors including the new Lacringi recruits. Nevertheless, it was clear that Goar's Alans were the dominant force. There were probably up to 3,000 warriors, maybe more. Several of their number were the female Iazygi fighters we had seen before, and they caused quite a stir amongst the Vandals.

I believe Godigsel intended to move ahead with the invasion as slowly as he could. However, the arrival of the Alans created an impetus of its own and we began to build a camp across the river the next day. The rafts worked all day, day after day, ferrying across a wagon at a time. The Alans were experts at coaxing their horses onto the rafts. The herds of goats were shepherded by the huge Alano dogs that every family seemed to have. It took three weeks to get the travelling party across. In total there were over 9,000 people on the move. Godigsel took satisfaction in the fact that the huge body of people would mean slow progress across Quadi territory. It was already June when we left the river. Godigsel confided to us that, by the time we crossed Quadi lands and then negotiated the crossing of the Danube, a much bigger river then the Tisza, it would likely be early Autumn. This calculation pleased him for he was confident that Alaric would be fighting the Roman field army in northern Italy by then. Godigsel had long been clear that he wanted Gisselitta, Fredo and me to go with him on the journey, nevertheless Gibamundus protested that it was too dangerous a venture for youngsters like us. Godigsel insisted and explained to his father that Gisselitta's tactical insight was now something he valued. Fredo was needed to liaise with Marobus and the Quadi and my position at my brother's side was never challenged.

Our journey to Raetia would take several months and it became an education of a different kind. We learned to live off the land, to make our provisions last and not complain of hunger, always to camp near water and most importantly to care for our horses. We only had one horse each unlike the Alan warriors who had at least two each. This meant regular periods of walking for us as, hardy as Alan mounts were, they could not be ridden all day. The importance of horses to a people on the move was fundamental. It was the most important lesson we learned on the trail to Raetia.

☩

Yannus had a question about the Alan wagons. "Master did the Alans use their horses to pull the wagons?"

No, the Alans valued their horses too highly to allow them to be draft animals. They used water buffalo to pull the wagons. Buffalo are extremely useful animals providing milk and meat. They have strength and endurance and can generally move faster than the oxen the Vandals and the Sava valley Alans used. A few years later, the Vandals' wagon train travelled together with the Alans' wagons, and we found the Alans were able to travel faster because of the buffalo.

☩ ☩ ☩

Chapter 10

The Raetian campaign of 401

For the first two days we were still in Vandal territory as we progressed north along the west bank of the Tisza. Despite the use of buffalo to pull the Alan wagons, progress was slow. The Vandal villages we passed seemed to be flourishing and there were no signs of Goth or Hun attacks on this side of the river. We bought whatever surplus food the villagers had to offer but the settlements were too small for us to camp at. The Alans, perhaps more used to moving camps, broke out into several separate groups based on their original communities. The Lacringi likewise formed their own convoy. At night, the wagons of each group were formed into a circle with the herds close by. The campfires of the separate groups could be seen over a wide area at night. Alan bands of thirty or forty warriors ranged far and wide of the convoys scouting out the terrain and hunting for game. The Alano hunting dogs proved their worth and we regretted not having brought our own dogs with us.

Godigsel broke the Vandal warband in two with half forming the vanguard. We accompanied Godigsel and Marobus in this leading group whilst Guntha commanded the rear guard. Within a few days we were leaving the Vandal villages behind us. There were no roads as such just rough tracks, but Marobus was familiar with which track led to the first Quadi village. Wherever there was good farmland and access to water there seemed to be a village. Often there were several villages in one small area and then none for long stretches as we passed through huge forests or over hilly terrain. Each grouping of villages seemed to belong to a separate Quadi tribe.

Marobus explained that the different tribes were largely independent and that there was no overall tribal chieftain at that time. Marobus' own village and tribe were to the south near the Danube, and it was there he expected the most support for the invasion. His tribe, it seemed, were used to small raids across the river. It was my belief that he told us this, in part, to explain the lack of enthusiasm from the young men of the first few villages we passed to join us. The villages themselves were not dissimilar to the Vandal villages, with long houses dominating the community. Farming seemed more intensive than the Vandals were used to, with pigs the most common animal kept. The villagers were fascinated to see so many different people passing by. They were amazed at the number of horses we had, and we could not help but notice how few the villagers had.

Feeding such a large body of people was, of course, a concern. The Alans were happy to trade a few horses for some pigs all of which were slaughtered and consumed that day. Godigsel and Goar repeatedly warned their warriors not to steal from the villagers, whilst Marobus implored each village headman to trade whatever food surplus they had. Generally, the villages received us well; however the meetings with tribal chieftains were more tense. The chieftains, no doubt, had to play up to their oathsworn and seemed quite confrontational when introduced to Godigsel and Goar. Fortunately, both men could be diplomatic when they needed to be and the gift of a horse or a sword smoothed the way. One such incident prompted Marobus to tell us of a time when his grandfather had accompanied a Quadi chieftain to a treaty meeting with the emperor Valentinian.

"The Quadi leader was so insolent and rude when he met Valentinian that the shock of his behaviour caused the emperor to have a stroke and fall down dead!"

We suffered two days of continuous rain and every one of us became a little depressed at our inability to stay dry. Gisselitta noticed that the Alans seemed to cope with the conditions much better than us. They greased their cloaks and leather hats with goat fat, and it prevented the rain seeping through. It didn't smell nice, but it kept you dry.

Marobus said that the constant rain was the curse of the Quadi gods. He told us that during the

Marcomanni wars the Quadi had defeated a Roman legion who were forced to surrender because of the lack of water. Before the surrender could happen, the heavens opened, the Romans were refreshed, and they fought on to win the battle.

Marobus insisted we make a sacrifice to the Quadi God of rain, preferably a human sacrifice. Godigsel and Goar both refused to countenance such a sacrifice and Marobus had to make do with a goat. It seems that the Quadi rain god was happy with the goat sacrifice for the next day brought sunshine and we all dried out.

Our fortunes seemed to improve too, as at the next village the tribal chieftain met us with a band of warriors all keen to join us. From that point on, small bands of Quadi converged on our convoys from various directions, all wanting to cross the river with us.

Finally, we reached Marobus' tribal area only a day from the river. Marobus' village was by far the largest and wealthiest we had seen in Quadi lands with plenty of slaves working in the fields and preparing and serving food. Marobus explained that the Quadi word for slave was thrall and that capturing thralls was one of the main objectives when they raided across the river. With the river only a few hours away, the evening discussions centred on how to make the crossing.

Marobus confirmed that his Quadi knew the best area to cross. They had many boats hidden along the shore for when they raided. The river was not that wide at this point, only 250 metres. However, the current was strong. The Alans reported that they had scouted along the river as far up-stream as Lentia and as far downstream as Lauriacum. As we already knew, there was a large legionary fort at Lauriacum dating from the Marcomanni wars. We were in a good area to cross and the Roman road from Lauriacum to Augusta Vindelicum would lead us into the heart of Raetia.

The question remained as to how to get the wagons and horses across. The Quadi did not have horses when they raided so it was a new problem for them. Godigsel reminded us of how we had crossed the Tisza.

"We have to construct a fleet of rafts to carry the wagons and the horses across. There are plenty of trees to fell on both sides of the river. We need to send an advance party across the river in the boats available, both to secure the area and also to establish raft building camps on the far side."

Gisselitta pointed out the obvious dangers.

"So much raft building activity along both banks of the river will be seen by passing river craft and then reported to the legionary fortress."

Godigsel conceded the point.

"It is impossible to hide 9,000 people on the move. The whole province will know we are coming. Let's just hope the Roman field army is engaged defending Italy from Alaric's Goths."

Goar said he would send out scouting parties as soon as his horses were across the river. They would discover what Roman forces might oppose us. The biggest worry was the strength of the legionary forces in Lauriacum and what they might do to oppose the crossing. We would be vulnerable when our forces were split with only half across the river. Gisselitta proposed that he and I, along with Fredo, should go into the *vicus*, the settlement around the fort, and find out from the locals what we could about the soldiers based there. I was a Roman after all and as youngsters we should not attract undue attention.

Godigsel would never have considered the idea had we not had the experience of riding into the camp of Radagarius on our own. Our Vandal guards and Fredo's Quadi guard took us as close to the town as they could and then hid themselves and our horses while we went into the town. I kept my horse and rode with Gisselitta and Fredo walking behind me. I planned to pose as a young Roman noble with Gisselitta acting as my servant and Fredo as my guard.

Two roads led out of the southern gate of the fortress. Smaller roads crisscrossed the main roads to form a quite sizable town. Settlements of this size were called *canaba* if, indeed, they had not been granted city status. The term *vicus* applied to the smaller settlements that grew up around much simpler Roman forts. The legionary fortress at

Lauriacum had huge walls with turrets on each corner. We headed for the food market, the *forum venale*, with food on our minds although it was also an ideal place to get information. After we had gorged ourselves on delicious meat pies, we noticed a centurion approaching the stall with a similar objective. We could see the insignia of *Legia II Italica* and presumed he must be based at the fortress.

I spoke in my best formal Latin and tried to sound the confident young noble I hope I appeared to be.

"These are delicious meat pies. I recommend them."

The centurion, noting the quality of my speech, replied with appropriate deference.

"Indeed they are, young lord. I should know for my woman runs this stall."

"Then you must be with the garrison here at Lauriacum. You are the *Italica* are you not?"

"We are, my lord, and what brings a young gentleman like yourself to these parts if I may ask?"

"My father and our *familia* are evacuating the area. We have an estate outside Ovilava, and we have heard a large body of barbarians are about to cross the river and invade the province. My father is down at the port trying to secure a ship to take us all to Aquincum."

"Your father sounds like a sensible man. We have been aware of the barbarians' movement for several weeks. They are mostly Vandals and Alans. Thousands of then apparently."

"Will you not sally out of your fortress and stop them, centurion"

"We only have two cohorts here, young sir. It is barely enough to defend the fortress. There is plenty of room inside the fortress for the townsfolk if they attack the town. They are mostly our families anyhow."

My voice adopted a note of disapproval. "Surely you must at least send word to Mediolanum?"

"Yes, my lord, we sent a messenger over a month ago. We have heard that the Roman field army is already marching this way. They'll soon sort out the barbarians."

"Let us hope so, centurion."

We had the information we needed.

When we returned, we found that most of the people, wagons and horses had crossed the river. Whatever awaited us, there was no going back. That evening the leaders discussed the latest news brought by the scouts and us from Lauriacum. Despite the ominous news that we had brought back about the approach of the Roman field army, Goar was excited by the reports of his scouts.

"My scouts have travelled as far as the valley of the river Inn. They report that it is perfect country for our people to settle. There are grasslands, ample water supplies and steep valleys we can use for protection. The valley is wide and stretches for miles, much as the Tisza does. There is room for the Alans, the Lacringi and, if you wish it Godigsel, all the Vandal peoples. Your people could farm the land as you do at home. There are only a few Raetian communities living there, and we need not displace them. The nearest Roman fort is at Batavia on the Danube, and I doubt they will be any more adventurous than those at Lauriacum. Between here and the Inn valley we found none to oppose us. Most of the land we travelled through was desolate. The Romans appear to have abandoned this part of the province."

Crixos confirmed the report. "My scouts have seen this land too. It is as Goar describes. The Lacringi also wish to settle there."

Godigsel nodded his agreement. "We will come and view this land and judge it when we see it. How long will it take for all of us to make the journey?"

"At our slow rate of progress, I believe it will take two weeks for the wagons to make the journey," Goar replied.

"Then we must send out patrols to the south to search for the Roman forces that march to confront us. We do not want to be attacked while we are on the move," Godigsel warned.

"This is all well and good for you Alans and Vandals, but my people are here for plunder and thralls. We need to find a town to attack, for the countryside is bare of food and treasure," Marobus complained.

The Quadi warriors had continued to cross the river in small groups after the main crossing had been completed. They now numbered around 2,000 and Marubus was having trouble controlling all the different factions. Goar found a solution that satisfied Marubus.

"There is a town at Ovilava not too far distant. We Alans and Vandals will bypass the town and leave you Quadi to sack it. After that head back to the river and sack Lentia. There is no longer a Roman *ala* based there. It is defenceless. Then cross back to your homelands before the Roman field army arrives. Of course, you are welcome to come with us to the valley of the river Inn, but you should know that the Alans do not intend to return."

It was early September by the time we had arrived at the river Inn several weeks later. It was everything Goar had promised. The different Alan and Iazygi bands and the Lacringi broke apart into their original communities and began to build permanent camps at separate locations along the river.

"But Master what of the Roman field army. The Romans may have abandoned parts of Raetia but surely they were not going to allow the Vandals and Alans to simply take what they wanted," Manius objected.

You are quite right Manius, the Romans did have something to say about it, as we shall see.

Chapter 11

The confrontation with the Roman field army

The Lacringi Vandals and Alan warriors had only a few days with their families at the new settlements. The patrols had been tracking the Roman army for a number of weeks and it was obvious they were heading directly for us. Godigsel's warband was already assembled when Goar arrived with his full force of warriors. The two leaders consulted and Gisselitta soaked up every word spoken. My brother said nothing, but I could see he was ready with his own ideas if they were needed. From the scouts' reports we knew we faced a large force comprising three legions of Roman Gallic infantry, two legions of Germanic auxiliaries, mostly Franks, and thousands of Hun and Alan horsemen. The Roman legion of those times numbered only 1,000 to 1,500 men so our best guess was that there were up to 10,000 troops coming towards us. We sent word to Marobus, hoping he would be safe at Lentia on the river by now. Godigsel said that the scouts had spotted Hun *bucellarii* around the leader of the Romans. Stilico was known to have a Hun bodyguard, so Godigsel suspected it was Stilico himself who led the Roman field army. Godigsel and Goar were of like mind and Gisselitta was not consulted. There was no question of fighting such a force. This was a time for negotiation. Godigsel told Goar of his experiences at the Battle of Frigidus and they both agreed that Goar's men had to make peaceful contact with the opposing Alan warriors.

Before any such contact had taken place, we heard that the Quadi had been caught in Ovilava and were now surrounded by Hun and Alan cavalry from the Roman field army. The Quadi had fortified the town, but their situation was hopeless. We could not understand why Marobus had made such a huge mistake by staying in the town for so long. The combined force of Godigsel's Vandals and Goar's Alan warriors rode towards the town just as the Roman infantry were approaching. The Roman Hun and Alan cavalry broke off their encirclement of the town and returned to the main Roman army, with the Huns taking one wing and the Alans the other. With the combined force of the Roman field army arrayed before us, Godigsel and Goar both knew that they had to come to an arrangement with Stilico or be condemned to death or slavery.

Godigsel handed a leafy branch to Gisselitta and another to me.

"Come boys I believe you have done this before. Let's go and see what Stilico has in mind for us."

We may have done something similar at Partiscum but I, for one, was not comforted by that. The army we faced had overwhelming superiority and I just hoped that Stilico would remember his Vandal heritage and not treat us too harshly. Goar and Godigsel rode towards the centre of the Roman line with Gisselitta and me on either side. The leafy branch in my hand was held high and none seemed to notice how much it trembled.

Four men rode out of the Roman lines to meet us. Godigsel spoke first in Vandalic.

"My lord Stilico, it is good to see you once again. I hear you have achieved much since I last saw you on that fateful day at the Frigidus river."

"Godigsel it is you. I had suspected it might be. I hear we call you king now," Stilico replied.

Godigsel continued. "May I present to you lord, Goar, the leader of the Tisza valley Alans. And this young man is my son, Gisselitta, and the other my adopted son, Marcus."

Stilico nodded to Goar and both of us before he indicated the man, clearly an Alan, beside him.

"This is General Saul. Commander of the army you face. I am here merely as an observer, as I had heard the Vandals were on the move. On my right is Lord Velda, leader of the Hun forces here today, and on my left Lord Abtin, leader of the Roxolani warriors before you."

Goar acknowledged Stilico in Vandalic before greeting the Alans in Alanic. The Roxolani were an Alan tribe. He merely nodded to the Hun.

Stilico laughed out loud.

"What a momentous day for civilisation when a Vandal and an Alan representing the Roman Empire can decide the outcome of a confrontation with barbarian invaders represented by a Vandal and an Alan."

Goar's response was more serious.

"My lord Stilico, my lord Saul. The Tisza valley Alans seek no confrontation with Rome. We will gladly fight for you, if you will allow our people to settle in the river Inn valley. The land there is empty, and we displace no-one. We were forced out of our home on the Tisza by the North Danube Goths and the Huns."

Before Stilico could respond Godigsel continued.

"My lord, I have veterans here from Sirmium along with many eager young bloods. We would be happy to form an *ala* here and we will also fight for you. As king I cannot lead them but my second, Guntha, is a very capable man. I would ask that a small band of Lacringi be allowed to settle with the Alans. I will lead the rest back to the Tisza valley. In addition, my son Gunderic, who now commands the *ala* at Sirmium, could join your Western forces in the coming war with the Goths should you wish."

133

Stilico raised his eyebrows and looked to Saul for explanation before asking Godigsel what war he spoke of. All his earlier good humour had gone. Now it was Godigsel's turn to be surprised.

"My lord, do you not know? Surely the Trevingi and Greuthungi Goths have attacked northern Italy this Summer? We are here because we thought you would be too busy defending Italy. The Goths have assembled many thousands of warriors including Huns and Alans. Now I can see that Alaric waited until our forces here drew your field army across the mountains before he attacked Italy. I fear Alaric has played us both."

"So, it would seem," said Stilico as he assessed the situation. "I need to settle matters here quickly for we need to turn about and get across the Alps before the winter snows. This is what will happen. Goar, you will provide me with 1,000 warriors. They are to travel with my forces now and you will lead them. Your people may settle in the Inn valley. Godigsel you will provide me with 500 troopers. They also will travel with the army now. Both Goar and Guntha will report to Lord Abtin. Godigsel, when you return to the Tisza valley, send word to your son in Sirmium that his *ala* is now part of the Western armed forces. They will be paid in due course, but they should be ready for active service on my command. They can remain based at Sirmium for I intend for the whole of Illyricum to become part of the Western Empire once I have defeated Alaric. The Lacringi and any other Vandals willing may settle in the Inn Valley. Now what of those Quadi down there in Ovilava? Are they with you?"

"They were my lord. In the circumstances I believe we could persuade them to provide 1,000 warriors for your coming campaign should you wish it," Godigsel responded.

"Good. Make it so Godigsel and tell the rest they can go back across the river. They are not allowed to take any plunder or slaves with them. Lord Velda, you will supervise the selection of the Quadi warriors. I want the best of the Quadi, and I want them fully armed. The volunteers will take the best of the Quadi weapons. The rest can be escorted to the river. March the new Quadi cohorts at double time until they catch up with General Saul. Lord Abtin, your Alans will remain to supervise the organisation of our new Alan and Vandal warriors. Goar, you have one hour to decide your volunteers. Likewise for the Vandals, Godigsel have your man Guntha decide on his men but make sure they are not all youngsters; I want some experienced officers too.

"General Saul I do not believe we face any threat here and we have bigger fish to fry. Turn the infantry around and have them head back across the mountains. Send word for reinforcements to assemble at Mediolanum. Lord Velda and Lord

Abtin and their new troops will catch you up in due course."

With that Stilico concluded the meeting.

"Gentlemen I think we are done here. My staff and *bucellarii* will overnight at that abandoned villa over there. Godigsel, you and your boys, will join me there once you have dealt with the Quadi."

Gisselitta was delighted at the prospect of a further opportunity to soak up the wisdom of the most powerful man in the Western Empire. Stilico's decisiveness in dealing with an emergency made a big impression on my brother.

We parted company with Goar and his Alan volunteers and with Guntha and his new Vandal *ala* and wished them well. Before he left, Goar confessed that this was the outcome he had hoped for. Godigsel led the Vandals towards the town with the Hun cavalry following. He called Fredo to his side as we approached the barriers so that there would be no misunderstandings. The Quadi pulled apart the wagons blocking the main road and we rode through to find a worried looking Marobus. The Huns remained an ominous threat outside the town. Godigsel immediately calmed him down by explaining that the Huns would not attack if the Quadi agreed to the terms offered by Stilico. Marobus was pleased with the terms when he heard them. He had feared far worse. Marobus explained that the Quadi who were not from his own tribe had refused to follow his commands when he ordered them to leave the town. He had not wanted to split his force and so felt compelled to stay. Marobus declared that the volunteers for the Roman army would be those from his tribe and that he would lead them. As Roman troops the Quadi would have the prospect of gaining battle plunder and this pleased Marobus and his men. He was aware that Vangio, and his Quadi warriors at Sirmium, had done well out of their service for the Roman army. Those Quadi that had refused to obey Marobus would return home with nothing.

That evening we joined Stilico at his temporary headquarters. The Roman supremo was in good humour. Much as Goar had always planned to join the Roman army, so Stilico had joined the campaign to Raetia, in part to secure new recruits for his army. He explained that the Western armies were still recovering from the civil wars. It was difficult to obtain Italian recruits as the senators in Rome were reluctant to release men from their estates. The senate withheld funding for new weapons and training, leaving Stilico with little choice but to recruit barbarians, who came fully armed and trained. Godigsel listened carefully as Stilico explained that he had withdrawn Roman troops from the frontier in Germania to supplement his armies. Local *foederati* took their place but the line of forts between the Danube and the Rhine had been abandoned completely. The river Rhine was now the effective frontier.

Talk of river frontiers prompted Godigsel to ask for an imperial pass to allow the Vandals to cross the Danube via the bridge near Aquincum. Stilico responded that he could do better than that.

"I am sending an embassy to Uldin, leader of the Huns north of the Danube. Now that Uldin rules over all the tribes north of the river except the Goths, I must know what his intentions are."

Stilico called in two young men. The older was around eighteen and a fine figure of a man, who could have easily passed for a Vandal.

"This is Ardabur, and he is an Alan or at least his father's family were. He will not only lead my embassy to the Huns but also visit the free Alans of the northern Tisza valley. Ardabur's father and I served Theodosius together in the east before the civil war. We were good friends but sadly he was killed at Frigidus. Ardabur has been as a son to me ever since. He will attempt to persuade Uldin to turn his attentions south, to the Eastern Empire. If he is successful, it may well give the Vandals a little more time in the Tisza valley."

Next to Ardabur stood a young Hun of our own age.

"To make the embassy go smoother we are sending Octar, here, back to his father. He has been a hostage with us for several years. We hope the gesture might just influence Uldin to look to the south. Ardabur and his escort will come with you to Partiscum before heading east to find the Huns."

On the journey back to Aquincum we got to know both Ardabur and Octar well. Octar could speak Latin fluently and was thoroughly Romanised in his manner and dress. Only his hair and facial features marked him out as a Hun. Octar and Ardabur joined Gisselitta, Fredo and me around our campfire one evening and we took the opportunity to learn more about Stilico and life at the emperor's court.

Gisselitta asked, "When Stilico spoke with us he called himself a Vandal. Does he genuinely believe that?"

Ardabur was happy to answer. "He serves Rome and has known nothing other than a Roman life, yet he still retains a memory of his father's origins. His barbarian blood means that the Roman patricians at court have never fully accepted him as one of their own. He rules because he is the most powerful, he controls the army, and he controls Honorius. Honorius is still too young to rule but even if he were older I do not think the situation would change."

Gisselitta wanted to know more. "And what about you, Ardabur?"

"I am the same except my grandfather came from an Alan band north of the Danube. I don't even know which one. I am looking forward to visiting the Northern Alans of the Tisza valley. It will be my first time in an Alan settlement."

139

Gisselitta now turned to Octar. "What about you Octar? Have you turned Roman in your time as a hostage?"

"By the gods I hope not! I've been away for three years, but I remember everything about my family and my tribe. I am longing to see my two brothers again. I will change my clothes before I return otherwise they will think I have gone soft!"

Ardabur's comment made me question exactly what I was. My journey was, perhaps, in the opposite direction. My heritage was Roman but every aspect of my life up until then was making me a Vandal and I was content with that.

⚓

"Master, I believe I have heard of an Ardabur," interrupted Manius. "Was he later *magister militum* of the Eastern army in the 420s?".

That is correct. In fact, he delayed the embassy in the Alan lands for a month while he dallied with the daughter of King Respendial. They married and had a son together. They named the boy Asper which means "horseman" in Alanic. Asper went on to be the strong man of the East and could have been Emperor. Instead, he put his subordinate Marcian on the throne. Gaeser and I met Asper and Marcian during the African campaign and, despite being enemies, we all got on rather well.

In fact, you may have heard of Octar too, for he and one of his brothers later ruled the Huns for a short while. We were not to know at the time, but Octar took a great liking to the Tisza valley when the embassy passed through. It was partly his influence which resulted in the Huns establishing their main base there in later times.

Chapter 12

The return to Pannonia

We had been away from the summer palace for just eight months, yet it seemed like a lifetime for we had experienced so much. Tzason, Indulf, Traso and Coccas had not returned and, as far as we knew, they were with Alaric's army in Northern Italy.

Our mother was not the only one to notice the difference in both Gisselitta and me. My brother had been a boy when we had left but now projected himself as a young man. Gunderic was happy to accept him as such and began to include him in the activities of the *ala*. We both realised we had to work harder at our weapons training. Our experiences at the battle of Partiscum made it obvious we had to be stronger if we were to wield a full-sized spear and shield. Gunderic presented us both with a *spatha*, a Roman cavalry sword, which was longer and heavier than anything we had used before. We practised with our guards how to ride fully armed and in unison with the troop. The horses we had ridden for the last six months now seemed, compared to the troop's horses, a little small and we wished Tzason would return to help us find suitable new horses.

Aside from our own training, Gisselitta took much greater interest in training Wolf and Shirkar. He had regretted not taking the dogs away with us and had seen how useful the Alano dogs were during the trek across the Quadi lands. Wolf was now the dominant dog and was clearly aggressive enough to be a war dog. Tzason's dog Shirkar now followed Wolf's lead and, with Tzason still away with the Alans, Gisselitta trained both dogs together. Our lessons with Diomedes recommenced and Fredo and Ingamar returned to the summer palace for the winter.

A huge wagon park now dominated one end of the palace compound. Outside the walls we had a herd of oxen which were to pull the wagons when the need came. A warehouse had been built and filled with non-perishable foods. The wagons, oxen and warehouse were permanently guarded, for my mother had invested a considerable amount of my father's wealth in preparing the community for a potential move. In other times we would have been fearful of a raid on our resources from a Goth warband but the war we knew to be taking place in northern Italy made that unlikely.

There was an air of anticipation around our community that winter as we waited for news of the Goth invasion of Italy. Soon after we had arrived back from our adventure, a messenger had arrived from Asphax to say that Alaric had finally begun his campaign. Asphax had kept his word to

Godigsel, and the absence of messages earlier had not been a betrayal. It was November by then, meaning Alaric had delayed for five months so that the Roman field army of Italy would be trapped in Raetia. He anticipated the Romans being tied down in a conflict for several months. As we knew very well, Stilico had settled the confrontation within a day. Nevertheless, the question remained as to whether the Roman army could cross the Alps before the winter snows. The cold weather began early in Pannonia that winter and we all assumed the Alpine passes would have been blocked by December. What that meant for our four friends with the Goth invasion forces, we had to wait to find out.

Rumours circulated throughout the winter months that the Goths had swept all before them in northern Italy. It was late April when we learnt the truth of the matter with the return of our friends. Tzason, Traso and Coccas rode into the summer palace with just their spare horses. There were no guards to escort them and that, and the absence of Indulf, told us all had not gone well. I had felt strengthened by my time away and I was sure that Gisselitta, Fredo and Ingamar had too. However, it was clear that Tzason, and the twins had returned diminished and were still recovering from the events they had witnessed. Coccas was struggling even to walk as he had suffered an arrow wound in his thigh.

It was Traso who recounted events initially. When Indulf and the twins had re-joined the Goths, they found that Saurus and the Greuthungi were in dispute with Alaric and the Tervingi. He said this was why the campaign had been delayed for so long. Gisselitta and I had our own views on that. Traso continued:

"The combined Goth army left in early November and headed for Aquileia which we put under siege. The walls proved too strong and, after wasting two months, we had to move on because we were running out of food. We broke into smaller bands and slowly progressed across northern Italy. There was no-one to stop us. We had the Alans scouting ahead, and we knew that, with the bad winter, the high passes would be closed. However, the spring melt meant our own progress was slow for every swollen river was an obstacle.

"We were heading for the capital, Mediolanum, and wanted to capture the city and the Emperor Honorius before the Roman field army could return. We arrived in March with no sign of the Roman field army and encircled the city. With the Goth infantry taking control of the siege lines we foraged all around the area for food with the cavalry. When we returned, we found that Stilico and his Hun and Alan cavalry had arrived unexpectedly and charged straight through our siege lines. Stilico was in the city.

"Our Alan scouts reported the approach of two Roman armies. The rest of the Roman field army from Raetia was only a day away. A second Roman Gallic army was approaching from the mountain pass to Gaul and was five days away. Alaric feared being trapped between the different Roman forces. He decided to retreat towards the coast and take the coastal route into Gaul and so outmanoeuvre the Roman Gallic forces.

"The Roman Hun and Alan cavalry came out of the city and tracked our forces. We made camp at Polentia. The warriors on foot and the baggage train were exhausted by the forced march. Fortunately, the next day was Easter Sunday so there could be no fighting. The next morning Roman Gallic cavalry appeared out of nowhere and, despite it being a holy day, we all went charging after them. Whilst we were away, the Roman Hun and Alan cavalry, pagans all, attacked the infantry and the baggage train and caused a great slaughter. My mother and my sisters were all killed along with thousands of others. They say even Alaric's wife was taken."

At this point Traso was overcome with emotion and could not continue. Coccas picked up the story.

"When we returned from chasing the Gallic cavalry, we discovered the horrible scene of the attack. Our foot warriors were still holding out, but the baggage train was devastated. We charged into the enemy and, as we hugely outnumbered them, began a slaughter of our own. It was during this charge that I saw Traso's horse hit by an arrow, and he went down. He fell under his horse and was trapped. I dismounted to help him but then I was hit with an arrow myself. I could not move for the pain. My horse ran off, so I stayed with Traso, who had been knocked unconscious, although I feared him dead at the time."

Tzason finished the account of the battle of Polentia.

"Athaulf and his oathsworn headed directly for the Alan leader, who we later learnt was General Saul. The fighting was intense for a few minutes, and I saw the twins' father fall during the fighting. He fought bravely to defend Athaulf to the end. The Roman Huns and Alans managed to break away and flee. My father sent me and some other boys to search the baggage train for survivors. He himself led an attack on the fleeing General Saul and his men. I did not see it, but they say he sent his javelin into General Saul's back and killed him. Saul's men turned back and killed my father and many of his men.

"As I rode across the battlefield to the baggage train, I came across Coccas lying next to his brother with a Hun arrow sticking out of his leg. The battlefield was ours, so I was able to organise help and horses for the twins. Traso soon came round after we lifted the horse off him, and we treated Coccas' wound as best we could."

Tzason told us he and the twins joined the remaining Alans in breaking away from the Goths. At the first camp the Sava valley Alans elected a new leader. The general feeling amongst the warriors was that their prospects would be better with the Romans than against them. They felt that the Goths were a spent force. The Roman Alans had lost a lot of men at the battle and would be glad of experienced recruits, but the presence of Tzason was a problem. Everyone believed his father, Asphax, had killed the great Alan general, Saul. Traso and Coccas were a problem too; they were Goths. The Sava valley Alans resolved to approach the Roman Alans the next day and offer their services. That night Safrax brought the boys spare horses and together they slipped away from the Alan camp and began the long ride back to the summer palace. Safrax had left the boys in sight of the summer palace to return to the Alans' Sava River camp and find Tzason's mother and sister.

Later we pieced together the rest of the Goth campaign. After the battle, the Goths retreated to the East, as an entirely mounted force. There were so many spare horses after the battle that all the surviving foot warriors found a mount. The Roman infantry pursued them but very quickly lost touch. Nevertheless, scouts tracked the movement of the Goths as they crossed northern Italy.

When Alaric turned his forces to the north, threatening to invade Noricum, Stilico was forced to intervene. In June, the Romans brought the Goths to battle again near Verona. The Goth attacks on the Roman infantry lines proved ineffective and the Goths were forced to retreat so that they could make a last stand on a hill outside of the city. They say that Stilico could have destroyed Alaric's remaining forces that day, but he chose not to. It is rumoured that the Roman Alans refused to fight. Whether the Sava valley Alans influenced that decision we will never know. Saurus took the opportunity to transfer the allegiance of his followers to the Western Roman army as he had planned the previous year.

Despite his weak position, Alaric was treated generously by Stilico. He was appointed *magister militum* for Illyricum for the Western Empire and was allowed to resettle in Pannonia. As a part of the treaty, he received Roman hostages including Aetius who, as you know, spent two months with us at the summer palace the following year.

Alaric returned to Pannonia later in the year but settled in an area much further south, near Illyria, than they had previously occupied. We presumed, and hoped, that Indulf was alive and well and living with the Trevingi. We had no news of him, and Traso and Coccas, still recovering from the loss of their entire family, showed no interest in finding him.

The events of that year brought a period of peace. The Trevingi needed to recover their strength after the losses they had suffered, and it took them several years to do so. Bizarrely both the Vandal *ala* at Sirmium and Alaric's Trevingi Goths were now part of the Western Roman forces whereas earlier they had both been designated Eastern Empire forces.

Yet no instruction came from Alaric, as *magister militum* for our area, or from Stilico. Gunderic was happy to let sleeping dogs lie. Even the threat from the northeast presented by Uldin's Huns both to us in Pannonia and to the Vandals in the Tisza valley seemed to lessen. Whether the embassy of Ardurbur was the reason for that we did not know at the time. The rumours on the river, which circulated down to us, were that the Huns were concentrating their forces on subduing a powerful tribe to the north. In later years, the Sciri featured as major allies of the Huns.

The peaceful times were enjoyed by everyone even though none thought it would last. Everyone except my mother, Flavia. She was hugely frustrated that Godigsel remained in Partiscum and had made no attempt to visit her since his return. I think my mother had put so much energy and time into making an evacuation plan that she wanted to put the plan into action whether it was needed or not, especially if it meant being reunited with her husband. Flavia did her best to bring Traso and Coccas more closely into our *familia* to help them recover from their traumas. Tzason too needed time to recover. With Flavia's support, all three asked Gunderic for permission to stay in the summer palace permanently and, more specifically, to remain as supporters of Gisselitta. That year Gisselitta became our leader.

This was too much for Yannus.

"But Master, when does Gisselitta become Gaeseric?"

It was that very year as we will see.

Chapter 13

A significant day at the hippodrome

Gunderic ruled the summer palace with a much lighter touch than his father had done. We still had Axxa and our five young Vandal bodyguards with us wherever we went. Since the battle of Partiscum and the invasion of Raetia we viewed the younger guards as our friends whilst Axxa was like an older brother. They were all dedicated to protecting Gisselitta, me and the others. So long as we had our guards with us, Gunderic would let us do as we wanted, which by this time meant do as Gisselitta wanted.

We were used to patrolling with the *ala* and, given that our group of friends and guards already numbered 13, Gunderic announced one day that Gisselitta would have the rank of decurion. Gunderic allocated 18 experienced troopers of Gunderic and Axxa's generation to complete Gisselitta's first command. With the experienced troopers' tolerance, we learnt every possible cavalry manoeuvre. On patrol we adopted a column of twos. The older troopers all had regular partners they rode with and, when necessary, fought alongside. Gisselitta assigned the partnerships for his friends and our guards. The partnerships were not random; the close friendships already existed. Axxa was partnered with me because we would always be behind Gisselitta. Kitan joined Ingamar and Otte joined with Fredo. The twins were split up, with Ulli watching over Coccas and Wada riding beside Traso. Skara joined up with Tzason while Gisselitta, as our *decurion*, had no partner but he did have the Alano dogs. Wolf and Shirkar were trained to run beside Gisselitta's Alan mount, and the horse was comfortable with their constant presence. We became used to riding with a spear and shield. The red cloaks that the entire *ala* wore made us feel like proper warriors. We hoped we cut dashing figures as we rode through the local villages although Gisselitta was constantly complaining that his horse was too small for a *decurion*.

Tzason recovered well from the trauma of his flight from Polentia and the loss of his father. Tzason's mother and sister now lived with Safrax at the Alan camp and Tzason became increasingly close to Safrax. After the Goth invasion had been defeated, some of the Alan warriors returned to their home on the Sava River. Not long after, Tzason brought Safrax and his new family to the summer camp and asked Gunderic if they might be allowed to live near the palace. It seems the returning Alans had ransacked Safrax's tent looking for any Fridgid river treasure that Asphax may have left with his family. They found none but it was clear Safrax, and his new family would have to leave. Gunderic was aware of Safrax's exceptional ability with horses and appointed him as horse master for the *ala*. Safrax, along with Tzason's mother and sister, became a part of the summer palace community.

The Alan members of our community grew steadily over the next few weeks as various young cousins and friends appeared to help Safrax look after the horse herds. They were mostly girls who looked to Tzason's sister, Farah, for leadership. I believe Farah meant happy in Alanic and, as long as she was able to work with the horse herds, she lived up to her name.

Traso and Coccas were slower to recover. They had, of course, lost their entire family at Polentia. Diomedes examined Coccas' wound and concluded that our friend would likely always walk with a limp. At no time did the twins show any inclination to return to the Trevingi or to find Indulf. We all tried to cheer them up whenever we could, but they remained sullen and brooding figures wherever we were and whatever we did.

Partly with this in mind, Gisselitta proposed that we not only go to the hippodrome for the next chariot races but that we also slip away from our guards, for once, to visit the stables and the charioteers. Our guards were as enthusiastic about the games as we were but would never consent to us going alone. Weapons were not allowed inside the stadium, although we knew the guards had concealed knives tucked into their cavalry boots. Furthermore, we had Wolf and Shirkar with us on leashes.

The games were as rowdy and loud as they always were. The Greens had a new driver, a man called Scorpius, who impressed us all at the last games. He could have won on his debut appearance had not the reigning Blues champion used his whip on Scorpius at the final turn. Scorpius' team were also new. Four beautiful black horses which people said had been brought in from Africa. We had good seats on the curve of the arena as Scorpius once again led on the final, seventh, lap. This time Scorpius anticipated the Blues' charioteer's move and evaded the whip. The Green team stormed to victory, and we cheered for all we were worth. Even Traso and Coccas were happy.

We had made our plan beforehand. As we left the arena, Ingamar went to speak to a group of adoring girls. After exchanging a few words with Ingamar, the girls very clearly beckoned to our guards to come over. We all made to move across with them but then when the guards were fully distracted, we slipped away into the crowds towards the stables. There were four stables, *factiones*, one for each racing team.

The stable guards would let no-one through, but Gisselitta proffered a few coins, and we were right there adding our congratulations to Scorpius. The stable hands were unhitching the horses and wiping them down. Tzason claimed that he had never seen such magnificent horses. Gisselitta found out where the black horses came from. There were indeed African horses but the Greens' *factione* owner had bought them from a specialist horse breeder in Moesia. When Gisselitta said he wanted to buy one, the owner laughed aloud and said a youngster like him could never afford to buy a horse like these. Chariot racing was a big money business and the horses cost a fortune. A winning charioteer could earn as much as 50 gold *solidi* for one race, an amount that would take a soldier 25 years to earn.

We were all in high spirits after we left the stables. Before we knew where we were, we found ourselves in a narrow street with our exit blocked by a mob of angry Blues supporters, *partisans*. Tzason turned around and shouted that they were behind us as well. We were trapped with no obvious escape. As the insults and racial slurs poured force from the Blues mob it was clear to us all we were in for a severe beating. I frantically racked my brain for a solution but could think of none. There was no negotiating our way out of this predicament. Gisselitta realised this in an instant. He took charge knowing that if you are forced to fight it is better to strike first.

"Form a wedge. I will be the spear head with Wolf and Shirkar. Tzason take the right and Fredo the left. Marcus behind me, Traso far right, Coccas far left. We go straight for that big lad at the centre, and we go now. Charge."

There was no time to think. We all followed Gisselitta and the dogs. Within seconds we were enveloped in a mass of punching and kicking. The ferocity of the dogs gave us a little breathing space but there were simply too many against us. Gisselitta went down under a barrage of punches with kicks about to follow. I instinctively dived over his prone body and shielded him from the vicious nailed sandal kicks of the mob. I held my hands over my head but felt my ribs crack from the savage kicks. It seemed to last an eternity but was, in fact, only a couple of minutes. Suddenly there was nothing. Fredo hauled me to my feet although I immediately doubled over with the pain in my ribs. Gisselitta jumped up from under me unharmed. I saw that we were all intact although Fredo was bleeding from a head wound, Traso had clearly broken his nose and Coccas was spitting out teeth. The dogs were agitated but lay at Gisselitta's feet on command. The mob had retreated fifty metres and stood staring at us. Then we turned and realised they were staring behind us. Ingamar and our six Vandal guards were striding down the street. The mob behind us had disappeared. Once Axxa had established that Gisselitta was unharmed and checked on all our other wounds he ordered us to retreat down the street. In those few moments, the mob in front transformed from youths looking for a punch up to men holding clubs and staves. Gisselitta warned Axxa to hold.

"If we turn away, they will be encouraged and chase us. We will have to carry Marcus, and Coccas cannot run. Let me confront them."

Gisselitta stepped forward with Wolf and Shirkar on either side. The guards formed a line behind him and drew their knives.

"I am Gisselitta, Prince of the Asding Vandals. My brother commands the *ala* outside of town. My father is King of the Vandals. We will destroy you, now or later, if you advance one more step. Go home to your families while you can."

The mob stood silent for a moment and then, one by one, they turned and left.

It wasn't until we were back in the summer palace that I came to understand the full story of the fight. While my mother fussed over me, and Diomedes treated my wounds, I listened to the various accounts. Axxa and the other guards stood before Gunderic with their heads bent low. Had it have been Godigsel they would have been given the lash. Before Gunderic could punish them, Gisselitta explained how he had tricked our guards so that we could get away from them and visit the stables.

A grateful Axxa then said he had witnessed our charge from the far end of the street and explained.

"Gisselitta was the spear head. He led the charge."

The words seem to hit a chord around the room. Gunderic nodded in acknowledgement.

"It seems our father has misnamed you, little brother. From now on you will be Gaeseric, Spear leader."

There was a spontaneous response from all present.

"Hail, Gaeseric."

Gaeseric responded by pointing at me.

"I only escaped unhurt because my brother shielded me from the mob when I was knocked down. I think he should have a more appropriate name too. He should be scutum - Roman shield."

The Vandal guards were not familiar with the Latin term and mangled it into Scuta when they all cried out.

"Hail Scuta."

Thus, I acquired my Vandal name.

We were all pleased when Traso spoke out.

"I fought beside Tzason. He held a bigger boy in a wrestling grip the whole fight without letting go. He hauled him one way and then the other to protect us both. He is a great fighter."

We all cried. "All hail Tzason the wrestler."

Coccas was caught up in the emotion of the occasion and could not help but join in. "I fought beside Fredo. I swear he knocked down six of them during the fight. I have never seen such skilful boxing."

The inevitable response reverberated across the hall. "All hail, Fredo the boxer."

Finally, the seven of us were left on our own with only our guards nearby. Ingamar was furious that he had not been a part of the fight. He had, of course, brought Axxa and the guards to the right street at the right time so he had played a part, but we all understood his frustration. Gaeseric, or Gaeser as we immediately started to call him, took advantage of the high emotions of the occasion to make a proposal.

"I would have you all as my companions, just as Alexander had his companions when he conquered the world. Will you all follow me?"

We all replied in unison that we would.

Axxa, Otte, Kitan, Ulli, Skara and Wada came across when they heard this and would not be left out. Axxa spoke for them.

"We would be your companions too if you will have us. We will follow you wherever you go and give our lives to protect you."

Gaeser accepted and we all swore an oath to follow and protect him.

Gaeser now not only commanded a troop he also had his own oathsworn. Gaeser took his position as leader seriously. He went to his mother and asked for coins to equip his oathsworn in a fitting manner. He had new blue cloaks made for us, that stood as different from the standard issue red cloaks of a Roman *ala*. The Romans considered blue a poor man's colour fit for servants or barbarians. Whether that was Gaeser's intention I do not know but, whatever his intention, the cloaks marked us out as special. He created a special type of cross and had the device painted on our shields. Finally, he promised we would all have black African horses like the Greens racing team although he confessed, he was unsure how that would be possible.

Manius posed the question before Yannus could gather his thoughts.

"The cross he created. Is it the Vandalic cross we are all familiar with? The one stamped on every horse."

It is the same cross, and I believe Hunneric has plans to stamp it on a new coin.

Chapter 14

A visit to a horse farm

For the next year the blue cloaks, as we became known to the local Pannonians, were a common sight in the countryside around Sirmium. We ventured further and further afield as our confidence as a troop increased. On the longer trips we usually took Safrax with us as his knowledge of the areas beyond the Sava River was superior to ours. He would often scout ahead to warn of any potential danger.

The Trevingi were entirely quiet during the years 403 and 404 and we never encountered any Goth raiding parties in our area at all. The Alan camp was peaceful, but we nevertheless avoided contact just in case Tzason or Safrax inflamed any old antagonisms. When the *ala* needed new mounts, we made the trip to Taurunum and brought back some of the horses that we had left behind two years earlier. We offered to pay for them as Godigsel had gifted them to Hildiger. However he refused to accept the money.

Trips to Taurunum became more frequent and we began a routine of leaving our horses in the fortress and getting a boat across the estuary to Singidunum. Gaeser was 15 by then and ready to explore every tavern and brothel that Ingamar recommended. Axxa and the other guard companions came with us. The relationship was different now that we were all companions and no longer boys. We could enjoy each other's company as one large group of friends. In the taverns it was usually Axxa, the oldest by far, and I who remained sober and kept watch for trouble while the rest had their fun. The taverns were also useful for picking up information and gossip from the river. When I think back now, it was there that we began the habit of talking to the ship captains to gain information.

The one subject everyone wanted to talk about was what Uldin and the Huns would do next. Most sources reported that the Germanic tribe of the Sciri had been defeated and now fought for the Huns. Some said Radagarius and the Goths would fight them next. Others predicted the Goths would flee West and attempt a crossing of the river into Noricum. The question no-one knew the answer to was which direction Uldin wanted to move next. Was it West into the Tisza valley or South across the Danube into the Eastern Empire?

It was in the Autumn of 405 that Gaeser announced to us that the troop would go on a trip to Vimincium, one of the main cities of the neighbouring province to the East. Moesia was a part of the Eastern Empire and we, in those times, were part of the Western Empire. We often went on patrol for several days at a time, so a ninety-mile journey was not that unusual. However, I am sure that Gunderic would have forbidden the trip had he known it would take us into the Eastern Empire. Gaeser had learnt the location of the horse farm that supplied the Greens *factione* with the black African breed of horses called barbs. He had convinced our mother to release enough funds from Godigsel's hoard to buy one or two of the African barb horses. Safrax joined our patrol as he usually did when we spent more than a day away. What astounded us was his declaration that he too would buy a pair of horses, a breeding pair. It seems that Safrax and Tzason's mother did, after all, have some of Asphax's treasure.

The horse farm lay just outside of Vimincium in the bend of the river Margas. It was a part of a huge *latifundium*, a Roman estate farm. The horse farm element of the estate was well defended with a low wall all around the stables and paddocks with towers protecting the main gate. We decided to leave the troop camped further up the river whilst Gaeser, Tzason, Safrax and I approached the main gates. The guards in the towers and on the main gate looked to be retired soldiers. They finally allowed us access once we had convinced them we were genuine potential purchasers with sufficient funds.

The manager of the farm explained that the owner of the *latifundium* and horse farm was a well-known senator in Constantinople. The farm manager took us into a huge stabling block where the long building was filled with stall after stall of magnificent barb horses. The quality of the horses was clear to us all; however, they were all of one colour, a dark bay. Gaeser made it clear he was interested in buying black barb horses, two stallions and two mares. We were taken to a second stabling block. Here there were around thirty grey barbs and fifteen black ones. Safrax and Tzason were allowed to examine the black horses closely and immediately Tzason came running back to Gaeser.

"I found him Gaeser, I've found your Bucephalus."

Sure enough one of the black stallions had a patch of white on his forehead just as Alexander's famous horse was reputed to have had. After some negotiation, Safrax was allowed to ride one of the black mares out into the paddock. The stallion with the white star reared up on his hind legs when Tzason approached. The manager explained that the horse had a very fiery temperament and was difficult to ride. Tzason calmed the horse and whispered in his ear. He beckoned Gaeser forward and together they stroked the horse and fed him crab apples. Finally, Tzason cupped his hands and lifted Gaeser up into the saddle. The horse accepted his rider and Gaeser was able to canter around the paddock. When Gaeser returned I could see his mind was set. Safrax too seemed satisfied with his choice. Gaeser proposed to buy the four horses we had identified for 20 *solidi*. The manager fought hard not to laugh in our faces.

"My young lord, I can sell four barbs such as these to the *factione* of Vimincium or any other major city for 50 solidi minimum. An aristocrat or senator would pay 15 solidi for one. I must respectfully decline your offer."

Before Gaeser could respond a stable slave came running to inform his master that more guests had arrived. We watched as a Roman officer and eleven cavalry men walked their shaggy Hun ponies across to us. Before he saw us, the officer spoke out.

"I am Ambassador Ardarbur. My family are friends of Senator Studios your owner. I would buy replacement horses for myself and my men. We lost our mounts in the Sciri wars. I need something to impress the authorities in Constantinople."

Gaeser stepped forward to be recognised by our old friend from Raetia.

"Why it is young Gisselitta is it not? You have grown into a man I see. And Marcus. This is well met. What brings you and your blue cloaked friends here?"

"It is good to see you Ardarbur. I am glad you survived your visit to the Huns. I am no longer Gisselitta but Prince Gaeseric now. We are here to buy horses for myself and my companions. However, I fear they may be too expensive for us."

"Spear king. A good name. It suits you well. Come Gaeseric, you can show us the horses in this building here. I am sure we can come to some mutually beneficial arrangement with the manager."

As we entered the stables, Ardabur's eyes immediately went to the grey barbs.

"Manager, I will have all these greys here. That is exactly the impression I want to make when I and my staff ride into the great city."

When we had ridden with Ardabur from Raetia to Aquincum he had a staff of thirty. Before we could ask, he explained that whilst fighting with Uldin and Octar against the Sciri he had lost more than his horses. He told us of how he had lost nineteen of his men.

"Those Sciri may fight on foot, but they are ferocious warriors. They delight in thrusting spears into our horses before dragging us down and killing us. Thankfully, they are now allies. So Gaeseric, which horses did you want?"

Gaeser indicated the black horses.

"Manager. We will take all the horses in this stable block. We can give you a chest of Sciri treasure. It contains some gold torques and arm rings, some jewels and lots of hack silver. I will commend you to your owner when I see him."

The manager shifted uncomfortably and tried to make eye contact with his guards.

"My lord, with respect, I know not the value of your treasure. I would need 750 solidi or the equivalent before I can sell you the horses. The Senator will have my life if I let them go for less."

Ardabur pretended to lose patience. He turned to one of his staff and barked out an order for his *bucellarii* to be brought before turning back to the manager.

"Perhaps I have not made myself clear. I will be taking these horses. You have a simple choice of accepting my offer or getting nothing. You are obviously unaware of the new situation in this province. My friend, Lord Octar, is the new power in this area. He has 2,000 Hun warriors less than an hour away. If you comply with my wishes, I will ask him not to raid this farm. Think of the horses as your tax payment to your new masters."

As if to seal the deal Ardabur's fifty Hun *bucellarii* rode up to the gates. Three guards dropped from the towers with arrows sticking from their bodies. The gates were opened, and the Huns rode in.

That evening Ardabur commandeered the manager's villa, food and wine and invited us to join him. Octar had ridden into the compound that afternoon escorting a sheepish looking Fredo and the rest of the troop. Fredo explained how they been surrounded and taken to Octar who, fortunately, remembered Fredo from Raetia. The campfires of the Hun army surrounded the compound.

Ardabur was quick to reassure Gaeser over the black horses.

"Gaeseric, the black horses are yours. I want no money for them, but I do want a favour. On my way to King Uldin we spent quite a long time with Respendial and the northern Alans. To cut a long story short, Respendial's daughter is now my wife. She is in Viminacium now with our baby son, Asper. I would have you travel to Respendial and give him the news that he is a grandfather and that his daughter is well and happy. However, you must also carry far graver news. My father-in-law and his people are in great danger, and you must warn them. My Lord Octar will explain."

Octar continued.

"When I travelled across the Tisza valley with the embassy I came to understand why the Vandals, Alans and Samartians prize it so. It is perfect horse country, and the valley provides the best grasslands in all of Europe. Partiscum is a fine town and makes an ideal main base, main base for the Huns that is. I told my father all about the Tisza valley and he will move there soon. First my father's warriors will sweep Radagarius' Goths aside. Your message to Respendial must be clear. His people must join and fight with the Huns or else they must flee to the west. Of course, you must also offer your father the same terms, although in his case he must give up Partiscum whatever he does."

Ardabur explained that his journey to Constantinople was authorised by Uldin. Ardabur had fought with Uldin and Octar against the Sciri and was now a trusted representative of the Huns. He had his own Hun bodyguard and was anticipating receiving a high military position in the Eastern armed forces based, partly, on his old family links but mostly on his ability to procure a large mercenary Hun force. Octar and his Hun army would stay in Moesia until they received a suitable offer from the Eastern Empire. Octar further revealed that his brother, Mundzak, had been sent north of the Carpathians with a large band of Huns and Heruli with orders to subdue the Siling Vandals and then circle south though the Quadi lands and back to Partiscum.

Before we left Gaeser bought saddles and bridles for each of the black horses. The ten solidi he paid was a generous price, in part, to compensate the manager for his losses. The stable hand who sorted the tack for us was obviously of eastern origin. He suggested a strange leather loop be attached to each of the saddles. He explained that the stirrup, as it was called, was used by the Parthian heavy *cataphracti* cavalry back in his homeland. The stability it afforded, allowed a rider to hold and thrust a much longer lance or spear. Gaeser and I had seen something similar, only made of cloth, used by the Izyages warriors. Always keen to try new ideas, Gaeser took the stirrups as well.

The next day we crossed over the Margas river with our new horses. We had pledged to visit Respendial as soon as the winter weather allowed. Our heads were spinning with all the implications of the information from Ardabur and Octar. Nevertheless, we enjoyed riding our new horses and experimenting with the new stirrups. They did indeed give a rider greater stability. Safrax was the last to be convinced but even he found he could throw his javelin further when using the stirrup. Each of the companions had his own black barb horse and Safrax had the two breeding mares he wanted. Gaeser's black stallion with the white flame on his head was the pick of the horses. The horse was aggressive with anyone other than Gaeser and Tzason. His fiery nature led to us all being a little wary of getting too close and prompted Gaeser to call him *Flamma*, Flame.

"But Master, although I am familiar with the stirrup, it is not something we commonly see in use today. Why didn't its use become popular," probed Manius.

It was something that always puzzled me. We, the companions, always used them but no one copied us. I predict that one day, every rider will use one.

Chapter 15

An emergency visit to the Tisza Valley

When we returned to the summer palace, we found we were not the only ones with news. Gunderic had had reports from both Hildiger and Vangio in the previous days. Hildiger reported that Goths were massing in enormous numbers on the northern banks of the Danube between Singidunum and Aquincum. He explained that it would be impossible for his small marine force to oppose them if they chose to cross. Vangio said that Hun raiding parties were being reported to the east of Sirmium. They had attacked farms across the area from Viminacium to Sirmium. Refugees were beginning to abandon their homes for the safety of the walled cities. He asked for more Vandal patrols to cover that side of the city. Gunderic was concerned that he did not have enough men to cover that huge area, and, in any case, it was Eastern Empire territory where he had no authority.

Gunderic was clearly troubled as to what the different reports might mean for the Vandal *ala* and the community at the summer palace. He agreed that Gaeser and the companions had to journey to Godigsel and Respendial as soon as the winter weather improved. Hildiger and Vangio had decided that for the time being they would remain where they were. What was the alternative? If a tide of Goths or Huns swept across the land, they hoped that the walls of Taurunum and Sirmium would be strong enough to protect them. For Gunderic, it was clear that the summer palace was no fortress should an army attack. Equally, to commit the community to travel across country in convoy was an extremely dangerous option. There was also the consideration that Stilico and the Western Empire might call on the *ala* to help defend against the Goths or the Huns. Vangio had explained that, with the population of the city increasing and food production in the countryside disrupted, once again life in Sirmium would become difficult. With Hildiger's blessing, Gunderic resolved to move the community to the fortress of Taurunum if the situation became desperate or if the *ala* was compelled to leave and join with Western Empire forces.

We spent several weeks waiting for the weather to break and at the same time training with our new horses and preparing for our journey. Gaeser wanted to experiment with a longer lance now that the stirrups gave us greater stability. Otte and Skara volunteered to work with the Pannonians, Jetmit the weaponsmith and Qendrim the carpenter in the weapons workshop to create a lance of eight feet in length. This was two feet longer than the standard issue cavalry lance. The ash shaft also had to be a little thinner to reduce weight and the metal head a little lighter so as not to reduce manoeuvrability. Gaeser was pleased with the result; the other troops, however, were sceptical of its effectiveness. The longer lance was difficult to carry when not in use and, for that reason, we did not take them on our trip north. Nevertheless, the companions persevered with practising with the long lances so that we could all thrust in unison from the height of our large horses.

I confess that when we rode out of the summer palace on our black barb horses one frosty day in the spring of 406, I felt I was a part of something special. Everybody stood aside to watch Prince Gaeseric and his blue cloaks ride by. With the addition of Safrax we were a party of 14, plus of course our two Alano dogs. We led our old Alan horses so that we could swap horses when we needed to.

We headed towards the fortress at Taurunum. When we arrived Hildiger was clearly proud of his son's position and appearance as a companion of Prince Gaeseric. He said he would do everything he could to help us complete our journey. Ingamar told his father that we would need six or seven weeks to complete the extended journey we would probably have to undertake. We were not sure, but it was likely that we would have to travel, not only to Godigsel at Partiscum and Respendial in the north of the Tisza valley, but also across the mountains to Silesia where the Silings lived before coming back through the Quadi lands.

Hildiger advised us to travel to Partiscum by ship since the lands across the river were completely flooded with Goth warbands and their wagon convoys. Although he had heard nothing from the Vandal town, he also warned us that it was possible that Partiscum had been overrun. To aid our return Hildiger said he would have two ships stationed at Castra Regina, close to the Quadi lands, in one month's time, in case they were needed. We left the next day on two ships of the Pannonian *classis* with the captains keeping us as close to the southern bank as possible. The Goths were everywhere along the northern bank felling trees and building rafts. We could not risk straying into bow shot range. Numbers were impossible to estimate although we all acknowledged that this was the greatest gathering of people we had ever seen and that included the Goth gathering for Alaric's election. There was no doubt the Goths were planning to cross the Danube in the next few weeks.

The following day we arrived at a much-changed Partiscum relieved to find Godigsel still there and the Vandals still in control. On the left bank of the Tisza, opposite the town, a new settlement of wagons and tents had grown up much larger than the town itself. The riverbanks were a hive of activity with rafts and boats constantly crossing from one side to the other. Godigsel's greeting was brief. He appeared to have aged considerably since we had last seen him. His father, Gibamundus, had died a few days earlier and was now buried next to the royal residence. Godigsel explained that, with everything that was happening, there had been no time to grieve.

"The Goths just exploded into the southern area in a tidal wave of warriors and wagons taking us all by surprise. It is impossible to count their number. All the southern Vandal villages had been abandoned. Most have fled here, to Partiscum, with whatever they could carry. But more than a few have decided to join Radagarius and his planned invasion of Pannonia and Noricum."

Godigsel had ordered a general evacuation of all the Vandal people for he had heard that a Hun army was moving West behind the Goths. Our news merely confirmed what he already knew. Wagon convoys were arriving all the time from Vandal villages to the North and East. They were immediately directed to the riverbanks and asked to cross and camp on the far-side. Godigsel said he would wait one more week and then have the Vandals cross the river leaving Partiscum empty. He intended to lead the people on the same route we had travelled five years earlier and establish a new base in the river Inn valley where Goar's Alans and the Lacringi Vandals were already settled.

Despite the urgency of the situation, the people of Partiscum all noted the new status of the king's son. That he was now called Prince Gaeseric was well known; however the sight of the black horses, the matching shield emblems and the blue cloaks created an impressive aura around my brother. We related the story of our chance meeting with Ardabur and Octar and explained our mission to Respendial. Godigsel had heard that the northern Alans were also preparing to move. He believed that they intended to travel north in the Spring, across the mountains, to the land of the Siling Vandals. If Octar had been truthful, then an army of Huns and Heruli led by Octar's brother, Mundzak, were somewhere to the north of the Carpathian Mountains. The Alans could only move slowly as they were burdened with all their wagons and families. There was a risk that Respendial might move into trouble if he went north. Godigsel urged us to travel on at first light.

"You must warn the Alans. We will travel up the left bank of the Tisza until the river veers to the east in that series of loops. I will have boats and rafts taken up-river as far as the loops and have a small band of warriors guard them for two extra weeks just in case the Alans need them. Tell Respendial he should send a messenger if he intends to move west and attempt to join with us. After you have warned the Alans you should continue north. With your fine new horses you will easily outrun any warbands you ran into. The Silings probably know what is heading their way but, just to be sure, you must get to them well ahead of the Hun army. The Siling king, Sigibali, was a great friend of your grandfather. It's important for him to know the Asding Vandals are migrating West and heading for Raetia."

We left the next morning and the land we crossed was empty. We passed two Vandal wagon convoys and urged them to hurry on to Partiscum before it was too late. On the second day Safrax returned from his scouting with a band of Alans. They told us the Alans were planning to move northwards and that they were to be the rearguard tasked with screening for enemy warbands approaching from the south. The northern Alans were a numerous people. We travelled on for two more days following the bend of the river. We passed over twelve different communities each with herds of horses, goats, buffalo, and sheep. Alano dogs challenged our own dogs at every approach. We were told that Respendial's tented village was at the centre of over thirty different Alan communities. When we had travelled to Raetia with Goar's people we had become used to the concept of an entire people on the move and the necessity to break up the travelling mass into smaller convoys. Gaeser and I discussed how a leader would move so many people. We remembered our lessons with Diomedes and how the Alans often splintered into separate groups. Would King Respendial be able to hold all the component bands of the northern Alans together?

Respendial was delighted to hear the news of the birth of his grandson but had no time to celebrate.

"I am pleased to hear that my daughter is well and that I have a healthy grandson. Asper is a good name. I will give thanks to the gods for the good news you bring. Your other news burdens me greatly. I must choose our course of action carefully or risk losing the loyalty of some bands of my people. Many warriors talk of joining the Goths in an invasion of Pannonia and Noricum. Tell me again every word Octar and Ardabur said."

It was clear Respendial had planned to move his people north. He had his patrols report the condition of the northern mountain passes. The passes could often be blocked with snow and ice during the winter. The patrols had reported a complete absence of Hun war parties in any direction. Our news that Mundzak's Hun army was moving north of the mountains gave Respendial food for thought. We relayed the information that the land to the south was empty and that Godigsel would leave rafts and boats at the Tisza loops for the Alans to use. Finally, Respendial took the decision. The Alans would move west and follow the Vandals towards Raetia.

We explained that we had a further mission to the Siling Vandals. Respendial insisted on sending two Alan guides with us to show us the pass through the mountains. In between the East Carpathians and the West Carpathians or Tatra Mountains was a river valley which wasn't too difficult to travel through even in winter. The area beyond the Tatras was Silesia named for the Siling Vandals. Much as he admired our barbs, he said that we should use our Alan horses as they would cope with the rocky mountain trails much better. We were to save the barbs for the flat terrain.

It took five days to follow our guides along the high mountain tracks and through to the plains beyond. It was hard going, and it was cold. We were fortunate in that there was only a light covering of snow. How the Alans would have coped with their wagons I do not know. Gaeser was sure they would have managed. He said that the Alps were much higher, and that Hannibal had moved elephants and a vast army across those mountains.

Our guides turned back once the plains were in view and Safrax rode ahead to scout once more. On the open grass plain it was easy to see the enemy from far away. Equally it was easy to be seen. Safrax, like all the Alans, was able to make his mount lie down simply by tapping behind its foreleg. Laying behind the prone horse the rider was hidden. As the horse stood once more the rider was already mounted. Using these age-old techniques Safrax was able to see a Hun warband in the distance without being seen himself. He raced back to us with his warning. We swapped to our barb horses and galloped away as fast as we could. The horses proved their worth and soon we were far away from trouble with no sign of pursuit.

"Master are those barb horses, the same breed of horse as we have here in Carthage today," asked Manius.

They are the same. After all, they originated right here in Africa. Of course, over the period of the great migration we had to change horses many times. Most of our Alan horses were left in Hispania, but we were always aware that we could replace them with barbs here in Africa. Those horses you see on the Alan horse farms in Bulla Regis are mostly crossbreeds of Alan and barb horses. Safrax proved to be remarkably successful in breeding from his two barb mares in Gaul and Hispania and then Kossus continued the programme here in Africa.

Chapter 16

The Siling Vandals

It took another three days before we reached the first Siling villages. Our provisions were running out and we needed hay and oats for the barbs. The Alan horses seemed happy to feed on whatever they could find. We lived off the land as best we could, with Safrax, Tzason and the dogs hunting at every opportunity. Both Safrax and Tzason were highly skilled archers and, with Shirkar to retrieve, we never went hungry.

The people and the villagers were noticeably less wealthy than those we were used to in the Tisza valley. We would gladly have paid well for any surplus food they had but they seemed simply not to have any. There appeared to be very few horses and finding fodder for the barbs became an increasing concern. We decided to ride our Alan horses until we needed to make an impression. In one or two places there was evidence of raiding. From the descriptions the villagers gave, there had obviously been Hun raiding parties in the area, and perhaps this explained the food shortages. The villagers were fearful of our approach until we were able to call out in Vandalic. Then the fear turned to fascination as they asked what kind of Vandals we could be with our fine clothes, weapons, and horses. We asked for directions to the king and always received the same reply. The king lives on the other side of the great river. Godigsel had told us that the river Vistula was the most important waterway in Silesia.

When we found the river, we had to travel north for quite some way until we came to a crossing point where ferries operated. A newly constructed wooden fortress manned by twenty Siling warriors protected the crossing. The Siling commander made us welcome and we enjoyed wholesome food and a warm bed in the barracks. The garrison had horses and so there were plentiful stocks of fodder for our mounts. We learnt that the Silings had elected a war king and that both the previous co-kings, including Sigibali, had stepped down. As we had seen with the Asdings previously, when the people felt threatened they elected a vigorous, younger warrior as war king to lead them through the troubles. We were not surprised to learn that Hun raiding parties were the problem. The garrison commander sent a messenger to the new king to warn him of our approach and, the next day, insisted on guiding us to the main town himself.

We travelled north-east following the bends of the river. It was apparent that the left bank of the river was much more heavily populated than the land we had travelled through. Each village was substantial, and the number of domestic animals and the quality of the long houses suggested greater wealth. A mounted Siling patrol found us before we approached the town and guided us through the increasingly busy streets. Rakow was a much larger town than Partiscum and had a crowded harbour on the left bank of the river. We were mounted on our barbs and, as we neared the hall of the king, a crowd assembled on each side of the main street. Gaeseric was obviously the centre of attention. People seemed to know his name and called out to him. We all drew attention from the townsfolk, but the young women of the town focussed their attention on Ingamar, Kitan and the other Vandal guards by calling out and waving.

We were ushered into the presence of Fredbal, the new war king, and his nobles. We could discern the two groups present. The younger warriors were no doubt the oathsworn of the new king. The older men, the tribal elders, included both the former kings. We were pleased to recognise Beremut, the amber trader we had met in Taurunum, standing amongst the elders. King Fredbal, a young man in his twenties, greeted us.

"Prince Gaeseric, welcome to the Siling lands. I hear from my friend Beremut that Godigsel now rules amongst the Asdings. I hope he and your grandfather, Gibamundus, are well."

"Thank you for your welcome, King Fredbal. Sadly, my grandfather died a few weeks ago. My father now leads the Asdings alone."

"My condolences on the passing of Gibamundas. My father told me he was a great man, and we could do with great men in these troubled times. What news do you bring from the Tisza valley?"

"I bring grave news. The Tisza valley is lost. Goths in their thousands are passing through pursued by Hun armies. My father has no choice but to evacuate the area and lead his people through the Quadi lands to Raetia. Within six months I predict the Huns will rule in the whole of the Tisza valley."

"What of the Alans. Do they join with the Huns as so many have?"

"King Respendial is also leaving the valley and will, I believe, follow the Asdings to Raetia."

King Fredbal looked to his nobles and nodded.

"We feared as much. During the Summer, the Burgundians from the east passed through our lands fleeing from the Huns. They faced the Huns and their allies the Heruli and the Gepids in battle and lost decisively. Yet the Burgundians are a strong tribe. They could have defended their land if they had faced only the Heruli or only the Gepids. But with those devilish horse archers added to the combined force, the Huns and their allies are unstoppable."

This was news to us. We were unfamiliar with the Burgundians. Gaeser wanted to know more.

"How many are the Burgundians and where will they go?"

"We did not count them but there were many thousands. They took two months to pass through Silesia. They have heard that the Roman frontier fortresses have been abandoned. They intend to join another band of Burgundians already living to the east of the Rhine. They believe that, once united, they can force a crossing of the Rhine and enter Gaul to find a new home."

Gaeser replied. "It is true about the fortresses. The Roman leader Stilico, himself, told us that he had withdrawn troops from the old *limes*. The river Rhine is now the effective frontier. Even so the Burgundians will not find it easy to cross. Frankish and Alemanni *foederati* defend the river for the Romans. But what of the Silings? As we have told you, an army of Huns and Heruli, led by Uldin's son, is approaching your lands. Will you fight them?"

Fredbal responded. "I was elected to lead the defence of the Siling lands. We can field a fighting force of many thousands. The Asdings are a small tribe compared to the Silings. The Silings do not run. I intend to hold the Huns at the river. You will have seen the fortress I have had built to guard the crossing. We are stronger than the Heruli and, if the Hun cavalry cannot get across the river, then we can hold the crossing."

Sigibali now spoke. "Fredbal. It is good to hear your fighting talk. You and your mighty oathsworn are powerful warriors. You have the finest weapons, helmets, leather byrnies and good horses. You have fought against raiding forces with distinction but there are only a few hundred of you. Most of the Siling Vandals are farmers with poor weapons who must fight on foot. They have no experience of fighting in a battle. The last time we fielded an army was against the Langobards before you were born. I know, I was there. I do not question your courage, Fredbal, but I would ask you to reconsider your tactics for I fear the river will not stop the Huns."

Before Fredbal could reply, Gaeser offered his opinion.

"I have seen the Hun cavalry close up. They ride and fight like our friends the Alans. At the battle of Partiscum, when we fought the Goths, it was the Alan cavalry that won the day. The ability of the Huns to travel quickly over great distances will be decisive here. They all travel with two horses. If your army prevents them from crossing the river they will simply ride up or down the river and cross elsewhere. Their movement will be so fast you will not be able to react. I predict that, if your army fights to hold the crossing, Huns will circle around you within a day. You will be trapped with the Heruli in front of you and the Huns behind. What is more Rakow will be defenceless."

There was much nodding from the elders present. Even Fredbal's oathsworn seemed to take Gaeser's words seriously.

Fredbal replied. "I hear your words, Prince Gaeseric, yet to fight them on the open plain is to invite a defeat such as the Burgundians suffered. On the other hand, if we follow the Burgundians west, we will be vulnerable to Hun attacks on our convoys. Sigibali had the people make the preparations for us to migrate west before I was elected. Yet now it is too late. Our convoys cannot possibly move faster than Hun horses."

Gaeser continued. "If I may suggest Lord King. I met with Octar, another son of Uldin, in Moesia. I believe his brother, Mundzak, is under instructions to sweep around the Tatras Mountains and into Quadi lands before linking up with his father in the Tisza valley. I would not expect him to deviate from those plans. I would advise you to evacuate your people to the north and then go west. Would your neighbours to the north allow the Silings free passage?"

Sigibali responded. "We have good relations with the Thuringians. I sent a messenger to them last summer to warn them of this possibility. If we went north, then we would avoid the trail of the Burgundians. Their passage through Silesia exhausted the countryside of food. There will be nothing for our people to eat if we simply follow them."

Fredbal concluded the discussions. "There is much to consider. I will go to the sacred grove of the gods this night to ask for guidance. I will make my decision tomorrow."

Sigibali offered us the use of his grand hall for the night, and we had a very enjoyable evening there. Sigibali had a grandson named Scarila. Despite being as old as I was, he was in awe of Gaeser and tried to monopolise Gaeser's time and learn as much about the companions as possible. Gaeser had me talk to Scarila so that he could spend time with Sigibali's granddaughter. Dagila was a pretty, young maid of 15 and she undoubtably captured Gaeser's heart that evening. Ingamar, Kitan and the others had invitations to visit the halls of other nobles around the centre and I got the impression it was the daughters of the nobles who were behind the invitations.

In the morning we were summoned to the king's hall once more. Fredbal had made his decision. The Silings would evacuate their homelands and move north into the land of the Thuringians. He intended to have the people eventually migrate southwest to the Rhine. By the Autumn, he wanted to have a base near Mogontiacum on the Rhine. He asked Gaeser to tell his father that the Asdings would be welcome to join the Silings there. If Godigsel reached Raetia, we doubted that the Asdings would be interested in moving north to join the Silings. Nevertheless, we would deliver the message if we could.

As we made our preparations to leave, we explained our plans to travel south via the Quadi lands and deliver warnings of the approaching Hun army. Sigibali hunted in the areas to the south and explained the choices we faced. By following the river to the valley of its source we would avoid the forests and the mountains, but we would add another ten days to our journey. The faster route cut through the ancient forests of the uplands. The forest was so dense he doubted any army could pass through it. However, he warned us that brigands ruled in the forests and any unprotected travellers were likely to be attacked and robbed. It was clear that time was of the essence, and that we must choose the faster forest route. Sigibali was keen that we take a guide with us who knew the forests well. He was less keen when Scarila insisted he would also come with us. We instructed Scarila and the guide to each bring a second horse so that we would not be slowed down. As we mounted our barbs to ride away there were several tearful young girls waving us goodbye including Dagila.

Manius asked about the Burgundians.

"The Burgundians have a powerful kingdom in Southern Gaul these days. Their king died just a couple of years ago, and, I am sure, he also carried the name Gunderic, just like Gaeseric's older brother. I presume the Burgundians crossed the Rhine with the Vandals?"

No, in fact, they did not. However, after we had passed through northern Gaul, they did cross the river and insert themselves in between the Franks and the Alemanni. They became *foederati* but were so troublesome for the Romans that, much later, Aetius had the Huns attack and nearly destroy them. Those that survived were moved south by Aetius and that was the basis for the Kingdom of the Burgundians we know today.

Chapter 17

The Marcomanni and the Suebic Federation

The first two day's travel were relatively easy as we traversed the northern uplands of the Tatras. The land was heavily wooded, yet we were assured by Holz, our guide, that we had not yet reached the forest. At our evening camps we learnt that Holz's family were honey merchants. His family lived on the edge of the forest where there were huge meadows filled with wildflowers. They kept hundreds of beehives which produced copious quantities of honey. Holz regularly travelled from the forest to Rakow to sell the honey. He explained that our journey would be safe until we reached his family's land. After that, the ancient forest began. He called it the Hercynian Forest and claimed that it reached from the Tatras right across Germania to the Rhine. Holz warned us that we would not be able to travel very quickly along the forest trails and that, as we were a large group with expensive horses, it was likely we would attract the attention of forest brigands and outlaws. It would take five days to cross the thickest part of the forest and then we should begin to find Quadi settlements.

Around the campfire, Scarila was eager to learn the background of every companion. We naturally told him our stories of the Battle of Partiscum and the invasion of Raetia. Despite being the grandson of a king, he was, in turn, desperate to impress his new friends. He told us that he had been on a hunting trip to the area we were in where his father had killed a giant auroch bull, the size of an elephant. We would not have believed his boast had not Holz confirmed the existence of such creatures in the area. Scarila said that only the noble families were allowed to hunt them, and men were often killed during the hunt.

When we approached the honey farm where Holz's family lived we could see the beehives everywhere but no people or homes. Holz explained that whenever strangers came his family would disappear into the thick forest where they had their homes and only come out when they were sure it was safe. As he spoke, his family and friends appeared out of nowhere to greet him. That evening we enjoyed delicious honey cakes whilst discussing the safest route through the forest. There was only one main trail which led in the right direction. It was just wide enough for two horses abreast to pass along. Gaeser advised us to ride in our twos with our shields facing out to the forest. We would wear our full leather byrnie body armour and helmets. Holz believed he could lead us to a series of hilly outcrops where we could make a defensive camp each night. He said that he had travelled across the forest before carrying honey to the Quadi. One man travelling alone was safer he believed as he could simply disappear into the undergrowth at the first sign of danger. A party of sixteen with thirty-two horses was impossible to hide.

Holz and Safrax rode at the head of the column as we slowly rode through an amazing underworld of darkness and grotesquely shaped trees. Strange noises periodically issued from the shadows creating an evil atmosphere that filled us all with foreboding. At night we had four stand watch while the others tried to sleep. I was glad to have Axxa as my watch partner and hoped that Holz's offerings to his forest gods were successful. By the fourth day we began to relax sensing that the trees were beginning to thin and that, perhaps, we were through the worst. Of course, that was the moment we were attacked.

We saw and heard nothing of the hidden brigands but fortunately our dogs smelt them. The dogs began a constant cacophony of barking and growls. Their alert probably saved us from a worse result. As our eyes were glued to the left, the right, and the front the brigands dropped out of the trees above us. Their target was the spare horses, no doubt hoping to cut them free and ride back down the trail. Hunting arrows sprouted from our shields and a direct hit on Axxa's chest stuck in his body armour. Gaeser was on my right when suddenly a fur clad figure dropped onto his back. I sliced my sword hard on the brigand's neck and hoped I wouldn't injure Gaeser at the same time. The fur clad creature fell away, and several others were similarly despatched by the companions. Scarila was exultant after he nearly decapitated a brigand attempting to steal his spare horse. It was all over in a couple of minutes. The brigands got away with two spare Alan horses from the back of the column. Axxa made a great display of plucking the small hunting arrow from his body armour and snapping it like a twig. I was unsure how to react to killing a man for the first time in my life until Gaeser slapped me on the back in his excitement and cried out.

"You live up to your name once again, mighty Scuta."

Fredo and Holz led us into the first Quadi settlement we came to. After what seemed quite a long discussion, we were given a warm welcome, food, and shelter. Fredo explained that there was some reluctance to feed us until he pointed out that we were sixteen armed warriors who could easily overcome any resistance the villagers might offer. In the morning Holz began his journey back to the honey farm. He left with our thanks and a gold *solidus* for his trouble. We were not too surprised when Scarila insisted he would continue with us. Indeed, we were pleased as he had become a popular member of our group during the journey from Raknow.

We doubted that a Hun army could follow our route through the ancient forest but nevertheless we did warn the villagers of the possibility. They seemed unconcerned. No doubt, much like the honey farmers, they would disappear into the forest at the first sign of trouble. The headman said it was for the tribal chief to confront any invaders and he gave us directions to the chief's settlement.

Two days later we found the main settlement of the northern Quadi. The small town seemed prosperous with farms and longhouses strung along the floor of a wide valley either side of a small river. The local chieftain, Vannius, styled himself king of the northern Quadi. He took our news of the possibility of a Hun army sweeping down the valley very seriously. He was convinced an army from the north would have to come in his direction to avoid the mountains and forests. The reputation of the Huns had spread far, and the availability of food, grazing and water in the valley made the town an obvious target.

To our eyes the town had no defensive structures at all. Vannius claimed he could field an army of 1,500 warriors and that he could fortify the main town with barriers and wagons. Gaeser delicately advised the king that, even if they could protect the town, the rest of the valley would be devastated. Vannius nodded his agreement and explained his difficult position.

"I have few choices. If I fight the Huns they will probably destroy us all. If I submit to them I become their vassal. They will still strip the valley of food, enslave my people, and make us warriors fight for them. If I call for support from the southern Quadi I doubt they will respond. My only hope is the new high king of the Suebic federation, Hermeric, leader of the Marcomanni."

We were told that the high king was based at Castra Regina and could raise a mighty army should he choose to. Vannius resolved to send scouts north to watch for the Huns and to send messengers to Hermeric asking for help. We were heading for Castra Regina to meet the ships Hildiger had promised to have waiting for us. We could take the message as fast as any messenger. Vannius said he would send one of his oathsworn bodyguards along with us. Gaeser told Vannius of the plans of the Burgundians and the Siling Vandals to see if Vannius would consider the option of moving his people west. Gaeser added that he expected the Huns to turn east once they were into the Quadi lands so that they could link up with Uldin in the Tisza valley. I could see, and understand, the reluctance of the Quadi leader to consider moving his people out of their homeland. Yet, just as the Vandals and Alans had been forced to move, I could see no alternative for Vannius' people. We left the next morning not knowing what would happen to the northern Quadi.

We rode to the west as swiftly as we could. After the first day the Quadi messenger had to swap to an Alan horse as his own horse was struggling to keep up. We had a three-day journey to reach the Danube and the main city of the Marcomanni. When we camped, Fredo and Ingamar spoke with the Quadi warrior and learnt more about the Suebic federation and the new high king. The federation comprised many tribes; from the Langobards and Thuringians to the north, to the Alemanni in the south. The Marcomanni had a strong royal family and had provided the high king for the federation for several generations. The federation was a loose organisation and the high king had little real influence on the tribes living far away. The Quadi, with no central structure of their own, were the only tribe that the high king could directly influence. Equally the Quadi looked to the Marcomanni for support and protection in times of trouble. Hermeric had only been twenty years old when he took the throne on the death of his father a few years earlier. Yet, he had already established a reputation as a great warrior.

Castra Regina was a Roman legionary fortress which protected the most northerly point of both the river Danube and the province of Raetia. As we approached from a hill to the north we could see down to the river and the fortress on the southern bank. The square of walls enclosed a grid pattern of legionary barracks which reminded us of the fortress at Lauriacum we had visited a few years earlier. The remains of the old Roman fort at Partiscum seemed insignificant by comparison. This fortress was built at a time when a Roman legion comprised 5,000 legionaries. Substantial settlements stretched out along the river on both sides of the fortress. We crossed the Danube via two bridges and an island in the middle of the river. We were delighted to see two *laburnae* of the Pannonia *classis* tied up to the wharfs alongside the river. Ingamar left us at the fortress gates to talk to the Alemanni *ripenses*. Marcomanni warriors guarded the main gate but let us pass without challenge. We headed straight up the main street to the old *principia,* the headquarters building of a legion fortress. The building now functioned as the palace of Hermeric. We understood that the last Roman soldiers had been withdrawn ten years earlier when Arbogast had recruited the garrison forces for the usurper Eugenius' army in the civil war of 395.

We were taken directly into a large room where the king held court. It was clear that Hermeric and his nobles were expecting us. It seems the captain of the Alemanni *ripenses* had been at the port for two weeks waiting for news of our progress. We let our Quadi warrior deliver his message from Vannius first. Hermeric was ready with his response and must have had forewarning of the progress of the Huns towards the Quadi lands. He commanded one of his captains to lead a war party back to Vannius with the instruction that he was not to engage with the enemy army if he encountered them. His message for Vannius was to evacuate the valley and come west. The Marcomanni warband was being sent to aid the process and form a rearguard in case of attack. We were all a little shocked at the decisiveness of the youthful king who did not appear to us to be that much older than we were.

Hermeric then turned to us and demanded our reports. Fredo translated his words, but we had already understood his intent. Gaeser began to speak in Vandalic but was quickly silenced by the king.

"Prince Gaeseric, please speak Latin. We all here understand it. The *ripenses* have already told us of the mission you were sent on. What success did you have?"

Gaeser told of his father's decision to evacuate the Tisza valley and of the northern Alans decision to join them. Hemeric replied.

"Yes. I have heard this. They are causing problems in the south of the Quadi lands. There isn't enough food to feed them all. Some of the minor Quadi tribes have appealed to me to intervene, but I will not. The sooner the Vandals and the Alans cross to Raetia the better. What of the Silings? They have a new king. Will they fight for their land?"

We ushered Scarila forward to speak for his people. Gaeser translated his words into Latin. The movement of the Silings away from their homelands was obviously new information to the Marcomanni court. For the first time Hermeric looked unsure and looked for support from his nobles. A younger version of Hermeric burst out in a rage.

"Brother, we cannot allow this! Just look at the trouble that eastern tribe of Burgundians is causing to our people in the north. If the Siling Vandals come south and join their eastern brothers, they will be a real threat to us. If the Thuringians have mistakenly offered the cowardly Silings asylum we should exhort the Langobards to attack them while we attack the Burgundians."

Hermeric pointed to the speaker and replied. "This is Heremigarius, my younger brother. Please excuse his outburst and do not take offence at his insult."

He turned to his brother and continued. "Calm yourself brother. The Silings are no cowards, and neither are they, or the Burgundians, our enemies. There is a bigger picture here."

Turning back to us he explained. "The Burgundians tried to force a crossing of the bridge at Mogontiacum three months ago. The Rhine Franks defeated them at the bridge fortress and now the Burgundians are licking their wounds to the north of us. They are desperate for food and have been raiding our villages in the north. I do not wish to lose warriors in a war with them so I will send them food on condition they stop raiding our villages.

"The bigger picture is what is happening to the south. A leader called Radagarius has led the Danube Goths across the river into Pannonia and Noricum in huge numbers. Some estimate there may be as many as 200,000 of them. They are heading for northern Italy. Stilico has recalled the army of Gaul to support the army of Italy in resisting them. There will never be a better time to invade Gaul. The Western Franks have already taken a huge area of Germania Inferior for their own even though they are *foederati*. The Eastern Franks, or Rhine Franks, have shown that they will resist a crossing of the river, but they are the only *foederati* that will. Our brothers the Alemanni are intent on taking territory themselves to the south along the lower river so they will not resist us if we decide to cross.

"I intend to call the Quadi and the other tribes of the Suebic federation to join us. We will make the preparations for sending a warband across the river to Gaul. I believe we can make the west bank of the Rhine Suebic territory."

We remembered the Goth warband leader we had met outside of Partiscum in 401. Now he was leading a massive invasion force into northern Italy. Our thoughts immediately turned to the fate of our families and friends back at the summer palace. Would the Goth invasion threaten our home? We had to return as soon as we could.

Manius interrupted.

"Master, we don't hear the tribal names Marcomanni or Quadi these days. When did they all become Suebes?"

Once Hermeric led his war party from the Suebic federation tribes across the river, the use of the old tribal names fell away. The homelands that differentiated them were no longer relevant. They were simply Suebes.

Chapter 18

The invasion of Radagarius in 406

It was the middle of May when we began our journey back to the summer palace. We coaxed our horses aboard the two ships that were waiting for us. Ingamar had made the arrangements for us to sail as soon as we were all on board. Within a few hours, with the wind with us, we were gliding past an estuary where the river Inn joined the Danube. A substantial town lay on the right bank of the Inn and a Roman fortress stood on the left bank where the estuary formed a pointed peninsular. The *ripenses* told us the town was called Boiodurum and the fortress Castra Batavia. As we sailed past, we thought we could see signs of Vandal presence in the town, and this was confirmed when we saw mile after mile of Vandal convoys along the southern bank of the Danube heading west towards the town. As we passed Lentia, we saw evidence of how the crossing had been made. Huge rafts lined the southern banks with a few still in the process of crossing. We called out in Vandalic to those closest to the bank.

"We seek King Godigsel. Do you know where he can be found?"

The Vandal tribesmen pointed back up the river.

"He's at the big town further up the river. You must have just past it. All the Vandals are to gather there. The town is called Boiodurum."

"And what of the Alans. Where are they?"

"The Alans crossed several days before us and, last we heard, were heading directly inland towards the Inn valley settlements of Goar's Alans."

We persuaded the captain to turn the ships around and row back to Boiodurum hoping that we could find Godigsel.

When we docked we found that the Vandals had completely taken over the town. There was evidence that there had been some resistance and that many of the defenders had been killed. Godigsel was easy to find as he had occupied the largest building in the centre of the town. He explained there had been little choice but to slaughter those that resisted the Vandal occupation. The town had food and shelter and the Vandals needed both. As it was, there were far too many Vandals for the town to accommodate. The wagon camps stretched away to the south of the town along the banks of the river Inn. Vandal warriors rode up and down the Inn and back along the Danube guarding against any surprise attacks on the people.

Godigsel was delighted to see us returned safely and we sat down to exchange news. We introduced Scarila as the grandson of Sigibali before relating all that had happened in Silesia. We explained that

Fredbal, the new war king of the Silings, planned to lead his people west to eventually arrive at Mogontiacum where he believed the Silings could force a crossing of the Rhine. We relayed Fredbal's offer for Godigsel and the Asdings to join him there. As we had expected, Godigsel was not inclined to turn north now that they had finally reached Raetia. Our news of the failed Burgundian attempt to take the bridge at Mogontiacum and the fierce resistance of the Rhine Franks merely reinforced his attitude. We swapped our information on the Suebic tribes. Godigsel had seen that some Quadi, but by no means all, were travelling west during the Vandals' passage through the Quadi lands. Many of the southern Quadi had joined with the forces of the Goth, Radagarius. We told of how Hermeric, the high king of all the Suebic tribes, was calling for Suebes to join his war party to take land on the other side of the river Rhine. Hermeric was ambitious to grab territory in the Roman province of Germania Superior now that there were few Roman troops to defend the province. Gaeser thought that it would take some time for all the Suebes to mobilise at Castra Regina. He believed that, when they did move, they would follow the north bank of the Danube south into Alemanni territory. The Alemanni *foederati* guarded the Rhine as far south as Argetorate and provided the *ripenses* of the Rhine *classis*. Hermeric hoped for a warm welcome from his fellow Suebes or at least an uncontested crossing.

When it came to recent events further south, we had to listen to Godigsel's summary of all the reports he was hearing. Several months earlier the Goths led by Radagarius, plus groups from many other tribes, had crossed the Danube en masse around the area of Aquincum using rafts and boats. Godigsel had heard that the defences at the Arpad bridge had been taken by storm with attacks from both sides of the river. He had no news on the fate of the garrison at Aquincum. Godigsel said all reports claimed an enormous number of Goth warriors and wagon convoys with families had flooded across western Pannonia and Noricum towards the Alps. Noricum had been stripped bare of crops and animals as if by a plague of locusts. The Goths had to reach northern Italy or else they would starve. He was hopeful that the Goth hoard had bypassed our community at the summer palace in eastern Pannonia.

As soon as the Alans had crossed the river, Respendial had sent out scouting parties deep into Noricum. They had travelled as far as the foothills of the Alps and found the tail end of three massive Goth convoys struggling through three different mountain passes. Godigsel guessed that, as we spoke, the invaders were on the south side of the mountains entering northern Italy.

Godigsel explained his plans for the Asding Vandals.

"We will remain here in northern Raetia, south of the Danube and to the west of the Inn. I do not believe Stilico will object. We still have Gunther's *ala* serving with the Roman Italian army and Gunderic's *ala*, no doubt, has been called to join them. Goar's Alans were allowed to settle here five years ago in return for their military service. I believe we can be secure in northern Raetia. The Castra Batavia fortress across the estuary is abandoned and that will make a good stronghold for us. The only opposition we face is at Augusta Vindelicorum, the main city of this province. There is still a Roman garrison there and the city walls are formidable. We will besiege the city and take over all the surrounding countryside. The city will eventually surrender when they start to run out of food."

Godigsel talked with confidence as was appropriate for the leader of his people. I was less sure this would prove to be a permanent home. Gaeser had similar reservations and I know he discussed the matter with his father. We were in between too many volatile forces, all with their own ambitions, for the Asding Vandals to be secure. The Huns could continue their sweep to the west. Radagarius seemed likely to conquer northern Italy unless the Romans could withdraw their forces from Gaul. The Suebes had ambitions to come south and take territory if Gaul was left undefended. Most of these forces were considerably stronger than we were. Maintaining our links with Respendial's Alans was important and, perhaps, joining forces with the Siling Vandals was not such a bad idea.

Godigsel wanted to give us instructions to carry back to Gunderic and our mother at the summer palace. However, it was impossible to know what was happening in eastern Pannonia. He thought it likely that Stilico would have called Gunderic and the Vandal *ala* back to support the Roman army in the war against Radagarius' Goths. Our mother and the rest of the summer palace community would be vulnerable if they remained at the palace without the presence of the *ala*. Equally they would be exposed if they attempted to leave without an escort. There could be rogue Goth warbands to the west and Hun raiding parties to the east. He urged us to return home as quickly as we could and send word of the situation via one of Hildiger's ships. If it was necessary, then Godigsel could send a Vandal warband back to eastern Pannonia to escort the community across Noricum to Raetia.

We continued our journey down the river Danube. As we passed Lauriacum we could see that the fortress was still intact and the garrison in place. Similarly, at Aquincum, the garrison still held the fortress. At the Arpad bridge there were Goth warriors camped on the island in the middle of the river. Goth warriors occupied the towers that guarded both sections of the bridge. We sailed through the stone arches with shields up, but no-one troubled us.

When we tied up against the moorings at Taurunum, we were greeted by Hildiger. Ingamar chose to stay with his family for the time being. We learnt that Singidunum was now under Hun control. Fredo left us to cross the Sava and visit his family in Sirmium. Local villagers told us that the city had been safe from any attack.

As we approached the summer palace, we became concerned by the presence of a band of Goths camped outside the walls. Gaeser and I thought it unlikely that they were a band from one of Radagarius' armies. We presumed that they must be Alaric's men come to recall the Vandal *ala* to the war in northern Italy. Traso soon put us right. They were Greuthungi Goths and, as such, unlikely to be Alaric's men and assuredly not from Radagarius' forces. Inside the palace grounds our mother led the swarm of family, girlfriends and servants that greeted our return. Flavia had adopted a different look in our absence. She wore a leather byrnie with a long dagger on her belt. Her hair was tied back, and she strode forward in riding boots. She said she felt it more appropriate for the leader of the civilian community in a time of trouble. Her two personal servants were similarly attired. Gunderic, however, was nowhere to be seen. We noticed a group of unfamiliar horses in the stables and guessed that we had visitors connected to the Greuthungi Goths camped outside.

As we entered the main hall, we saw that Gunderic was in deep discussion with a man who looked familiar. He had the uniform and armour of a Roman general but was clearly a Goth. We now understood that the Goths outside were the *bucellarii* of this Roman general. Gunderic broke away from his visitor to greet us before turning to introduce us.

"Welcome back, Gaeseric. You will remember Sigirus from the gathering of the Goths a few years back. He and his brother are both now Roman generals. In fact, Saurus is second in command to Stilico in the Roman army of Italy."

Sigirus rose to greet Gaeser in Roman military style, clasping his forearm.

"I remember a skinny youth called Gisselitta. Now I see a young man with impressive bodyguards and a more suitable name. This is well met, Prince Gaeseric."

Gunderic included Gaeser and me in the discussions. It soon became clear that Stilico had sent Sigirus to recall the Vandal *ala* to the main Roman army in Italy although that was not his main task. The Vandal *ala* would make little difference in the war against Radagarius' forces in Italy. What would make a difference was a Hun army and Sigirus had come to recruit them. Our old friend Ardabur was expected at the summer palace to broker the deal with Sigirus whereby Octar's Hun army would join the Roman forces in Italy. The very next day, Ardabur rode into the palace grounds accompanied by a staff of thirty. His Hun *bucellarii* remained outside the palace walls keeping their distance from Sigirus' Goths. Ardabur's staff rode the superb grey barb horses with which we were familiar. They looked magnificent. Ardabur was pleased to see us. We talked briefly before he went into a private meeting with Sigirus. He explained that with the help of the barb horses, his Hun *bucellarii* and his Hun connections he had made the intended impression in Constantinople. He had been appointed as *Dux* of Moesia. Of course, the *de facto* ruler of Moesia was Octar. Nevertheless, it was an impressive start to Ardabur's military career in the Eastern Empire.

While the negotiations were taking place, Gaeser and I managed to talk with a young Roman tribune on Sigirus' staff. We learnt that the Roman army in northern Italy only numbered 20,000 and that Stilico and Saurus had fallen back from the northern cities whilst they awaited reinforcements from Gaul and elsewhere. Radagarius' forces now formed three separate armies and were pillaging across northern Italy. The situation was so desperate that Stilico was allowing slaves to join the army. Stilico wanted to call on Alaric's Trevingi Goths but could not do so without losing the support of Saurus and his Greuthungi Goths. Sigirus' mission to recruit a Hun army was vital. They had brought gold for the Huns and would promise them Roman hostages and territory in Pannonia. It seems that our old friend Aetius was to be released by Alaric and handed over to Uldin and the Huns.

The negotiations concluded quickly and Ardabur sent five of his Huns off with a message for Octar. While we waited for the arrival of the Hun army, Gunderic explained his predicament. He had no choice but to leave with Sigirus and the Huns. He believed that the Huns had been promised eastern Pannonia after the war. The future for the summer palace community did not look good. He had, however, been able to negotiate the temporary release of Gaeseric's troop from the *ala* to escort the civilian population of the summer palace to Taurunum. Gunderic asked Gaeser to lead the convoy and wait at Taurunum for Godigsel to send warriors to escort the summer palace convoy to Raetia. Three days later the palace was surrounded by 5,000 Hun warriors led by Octar.

Before we knew it Gunderic, the Vandal *ala* and the Hun army were gone. Flavia wasted no time in organising our convoy. Everything had been prepared for some time. The number of Pannonians and others who were coming with us surprised us. There were sixty wagons travelling in two columns in a convoy of around 400 men, women, and children. They included Tzason's remaining family, Safrax with his horses and the group of Alan boys and girls who helped to look after them. However, we had to say a sad farewell to our former teacher, Diomedes. He said he was too old to contemplate a trek into the unknown. He had an ambition to return to Athens, but I don't know if he ever made the journey back to his Greek home.

We were worried that our numbers were too great to fit into the fortress at Taurunum, so we sent a messenger on ahead. He was to warn Hildiger of our approach and then continue to Boiodurum and Godigsel via ship. Our numbers increased unexpectedly when Fredo rode up to join the convoy with a squad of around 20 young Quadi soldiers trailing on foot behind him. There was never any question that Fredo would fail to join us but the stories he told of his adventures as a companion of Gaeseric had inspired several of his friends to follow him and the Vandals west.

Yannus wanted to know more. "What happened to Vangio and the rest of the Quadi garrison? Did the Huns attack the city after the war?"

The older members of the garrison were too deeply embedded in the city with Pannonian wives, families, and children to consider leaving. They had decided to stay no matter what happened. They had heard that the citizens of Singidunum had not resisted the Huns and, as a result, had been treated well. When, much later, the Huns did dominate the whole area the garrison never resisted, and the city survived.

Chapter 19

The beginnings of the Hun empire

We arrived safely before the walls of Taurunum. As we had feared, it was impossible for the convoy of wagons and all the people to fit inside. Flavia organised a line of wagons alongside the northern perimeter of the fortress. Our animals occupied the space between the walls and the wagons. Pannonian militia, Quadi soldiers and Vandal troopers guarded each section of our wall of wagons. Inside the fortress Hildiger and Ingamar gave us a warm welcome. However, it was clear that the arrival of the convoy presented Hildiger with plenty of problems.

We sat together that evening and began to understand the difficulties the Alemanni garrison were facing. By far the biggest problem was the lack of food. Trade along the river had reduced to almost nothing. The Huns controlled both banks of the Tisza River and the north bank of the Danube. A Goth warband held the bridge at Arpum. The port city across the water still functioned but the customs house in Singidunum was now run by officers appointed by the Huns. Worst of all there was a severe food shortage in the countryside to the south and west. The Alemanni garrison was earning no money from port duties and, in any case, could not source any food to buy. What little was available had quadrupled in price. The garrison simply could not contemplate feeding the extra 450 mouths of the Vandal convoy. Flavia was quick to explain that the convoy was well provisioned and would not need feeding by the garrison. The Vandal convoy's only need was security until a relief force could arrive from Raetia. We all lapsed into silence once the full dimensions of our predicament became clear.

The next day a familiar face arrived from his ship berthed alongside the *laburnae* in the fortress's enclosed harbour. The last time we had seen him had been in the Silings' main town of Raknow. We were intrigued as to how he could still be sailing the Tisza. Beremut, the amber trader, brought us all up to date with the developments in the Hun-controlled lands to the North and East.

"I stayed in Raknow when the Silings left. Plenty of others did too especially those too poor to have a wagon or horse. My main assets were my ships on the Vistula and the Tisza and my trading contacts. If I had left, then I would have had nothing.

"Mundzak and the Huns arrived in the town about a month after Fredbal had left. There was no resistance and life continued as normal albeit with Huns occupying the main halls. I managed to get an audience with Mundzak himself and presented him with an amber medallion as a gift. He seemed pleased so I explained I could get more amber if I had his permission to trade along the rivers to the Danube. He agreed on condition I brought more amber jewellery to him at Partiscum where he planned to base himself. He gave me a decorated staff with a figure of a bear carved at the top to denote my status as a Hun approved trader. I went north to buy more amber.

"Mundzak left a Heruli garrison and appointed one of the Heruli chiefs to rule in Raknow. Mundzak and the Huns left Silesia to subdue the Quadi lands. By the time I returned south, Mundzak held court in Godigsel's old palace in Partiscum. I went to pay my respects and offer my 'tax' of an amber cloak clasp.

"I learned that Uldin had left the Tisza valley to go back east. Mundzak was left in charge of all the northern lands. He controlled the Heruli in the north, those of the Quadi who remained in the west, his own Hun bands in the Tisza valley plus the Gepids, who have moved into the Goths old territories to the east. Mundzak's brother, Octar, is based in Moesia with the Eastern Empire's permission. He has a Sciri army based there, and it is those warriors that now run affairs across the water in Singidunum. Octar has led his Hun army west to fight for Stilico. The third brother, Ruglia, remained north of the Danube in their old heartlands and was supposed to rule there."

Gaeser explained that we had witnessed the meeting between the Roman general, Sigiris, and Octar's representatives before asking if Beremut knew why Uldin had left.

"Uldin's problem is that another Hun leader has risen to prominence in the east. Ruglia's authority has been challenged by a leader called Charaton. From what I understand Uldin had received a great deal of gold from the Eastern Empire to refrain from attacking across the Danube. In part this was why Uldin expanded his territory to the west. Uldin was also rewarded for capturing Gainus the Goth whom the emperor Arcadius viewed as a traitor."

Gaeser knew the story of Gainus. "He was an important eastern commander at the Battle of Frigidus. Stilico had him stay in the east and dispose of Stilico's rival Rufinus. He went on to be the strong man of the Eastern Empire but then had to flee during one of the anti-Goth purges. Uldin captured him, cut off his head and returned it to the emperor."

Beremut continued. "I believe that is correct, Prince Gaeseric. However, Uldin did not share enough gold between the Hun tribes left north of the Danube and especially with this Charaton. When Uldin drove Radagarius' Goths west, Charaton began stirring up trouble and threatened to raid into Thrace and take his own rewards. This was not a part of Uldin's plans or his treaty commitments to the Eastern Empire. Uldin has gone back east to reinforce his rule and prevent Charaton from invading the Empire."

Hildiger was impatient to hear of conditions on the local rivers and in the ports. The ships of the Pannonian *classis* had been confined to port over the last few months.

Beremut continued. "The Huns do not tend to trouble ships on the rivers. At every port you stop at, you must pay something even if you have official status like me. I sailed to Singidunum to sell my amber stocks. There are Eastern traders there who bought all my amber for a remarkably high price. I thought you might be short on provisions so I bought whatever food I could and brought it across the estuary to you."

Hildiger replied that he was unsure if he had sufficient funds to pay for the provisions Beremut had brought. Flavia immediately insisted that she would pay the trader as a way of thanking Hildiger for his hospitality. It seems that the treasure Godigsel had brought back from the Battle of Frigidus was not yet exhausted.

Later that evening Flavia took Gaeser and me to the wagon she shared with her attendants and Gregor. Gregor drove the wagon and slept underneath at night. Our mother sent her attendants and Gregor on errands and, whilst they were away, revealed the secret compartment where she had hidden Godigsel's treasure chest. The box was a Roman army pay chest. The treasure inside was mostly gold *solidi* and silver *denari* coins. Laying on top was a cross wrapped in cloth. Flavia removed the cloth to reveal the most richly decorated object I had ever seen. The golden cross was encrusted with what we presumed were diamonds and emeralds. Flavia explained that the cross had been displayed to the troops of Eugenious by Ambrose, the Bishop of Mediolanum, before the battle of Frigidus. When Godigsel and the Vandal *ala* captured the baggage train after the battle, they had found an army pay chest and captured Ambrose. The bishop had given Godigsel the cross in return for his life. The value of the cross was beyond calculation but only if sold in a great city like Constantinople or Rome.

Flavia feared that in our new home in Raetia, or wherever the Vandals settled, there would be no one to buy such a valuable object. We would be forced to cannibalise the cross for the metal and jewel content and thereby lose its unique value. Beremut's mention of eastern traders in Singidunum made Flavia think that this might be the last opportunity to sell the cross for anything like its real value.

We resolved to attempt to sell the cross in Singidunum with Beremut's help. Along with Beremut and myself, Ingamar, Gaeser and our Vandal guard companions made up the party.

Beremut said that the Sciri looked no different to Vandals and so, with regular clothing, we would not stand out. Ingamar knew the streets of the city well and Beremut could identify the richest of the eastern traders from his amber transaction. Beremut did not think that the easterners had sufficient guards to simply overcome our own guards and rob us and, in any case, he felt the prospect of making a ten-fold profit on the deal would be enough for them.

We docked at the port with an empty ship. Beremut was known to the port official and explained that he was buying more food from the market. The eastern traders had hired their own building next to the main market so that the whole transaction could proceed unobserved. Beremut negotiated on our behalf and was able to agree the sale of the cross for a huge amount of gold. The easterners pretended that we had driven a hard bargain. They spoke in Greek amongst themselves believing that none of us understood what they were saying. Gaeser and I understood them perfectly and knew that they were delighted with the deal.

We bought as much food in the market as the ship could carry, paying the exorbitant prices without a second thought. As porters carried the goods to the ship, we strolled through the streets reflecting that life in the city was just as it had always been. Food was in short supply and prices were high, but the markets were still busy. The churches were still open and Beremut explained that the pagan Huns showed no interest in religious persecution. Indeed, the choice of the Arian Christian Sciri to police the city showed some sensitivity. The streets seemed safe and calm, so much so that Ingamar tried to tempt us to a visit to his favourite brothel. Gaeser dismissed the idea saying that we were carrying too much gold to do other than return as soon as we could.

The arrival of more food improved the mood the next evening. Yet our basic dilemma remained. We could not stay in Taurunum indefinitely not knowing whether help was on its way or how long we could feed ourselves. It was Ingamar who came up with what appeared to be a solution.

"The river and our ships are the answer. We could use the fleet to ferry the women, children, and the elderly up the river to Boiodorum. We have sailed past the Goths at the bridge before without trouble. That way there will be fewer mouths to feed and, when the convoy is forced to leave as seems inevitable, it will be less vulnerable to attack. The fleet could even bring back Vandal warriors to protect the convoy."

Hildiger was agreeable. "The Alemanni women and children should go too. I believe it is only a matter of time before we are forced to abandon the fortress. We would need to use every ship we have here. The fortress would be unprotected if most of the marines are crewing the ships."

Gaeser said the Vandal troopers could man the fortress walls whilst the *ripenses* were away. Flavia was reluctant to leave the wagons and oxen she had assembled over the last few months and felt responsible for. Her own wagon, for reasons we now understood, was a concern. Eventually she agreed to sail up the river with the other women and children. There was no question of everyone leaving by ship. The convoy of wagons and oxen was a vitally valuable resource for a people on the move and could not be abandoned.

Two days later, after the arrival of a fleet *laburnum* from the north, we had to change our plans. The bodies of six marines were carried off the ship as the captain explained that the Huns now controlled the bridge at Arpum. They were forcing every ship to stop and pay a tax under threat of attack. As the marines had the current and wind with them the captain had decided to make a run through the arches. The ship had been showered with Hun arrows and, despite having shields up, six marines had been hit as they tried to protect the captain at the steer board. The captain said that, had they been travelling up stream requiring the marines to row, they would have suffered far more casualties. No-one contemplated sending the women and children through such an ordeal. In any case our messenger to Godigsel had returned on the ship with the news that a Vandal war party was heading south to escort us back to Raetia. Godigsel's message was that he would follow the Danube to Vindobona and then cut right across Pannonia to Taurunum taking the shortest possible route. That meant passing by the southern tip of the inland sea the Romans called Lacos Pelso. The Quadi named it the Platten or Flat Sea as it was known to be a very shallow lake.

Vangio reacted badly to the news that his ships had effectively lost their ability to sail north without confronting Huns. The link to the Alemanni homelands had been broken. After ten years at the fortress of Tuarunum and controlling the Pannonian *classis* it was time for the Alemanni to leave. Vangio's decision to join us on our journey north prompted Flavia and Gaeser to announce that the Vandal convoy would leave the fortress the next day. We would travel towards the Flat Sea and hope to meet Godigsel on the way.

Manius interrupted at that point.

"Before you continue Master, I wanted to ask about Attila, the Hun leader we have heard of. Was he related to Uldin?"

He was Uldin's grandson. Mundzak was never ruler of all the Huns, but his two sons did go on to rule. Bleda was the oldest son and ruled after Ruglia died. Some say Bleda ruled alongside his younger brother Attila. Others say that Attila murdered Bleda to become sole king.

Chapter 20

The convoy to Raetia and
the defeat of Radagarius

Before we left, Gaeser held a meeting where he went over every detail with the leaders of the convoy. Safrax and Tzason had been away for the past week acting as our long-distance scouts. They had already reported that the road alongside the river was clear all the way to Colonia Aelia Mursa. This was the better route as they had seen Hun warbands on the inland road to Sirmium. Safrax said the Huns now occupied the summer palace. It was 100 miles to Aelia Mursa which meant a journey of 10 days for our slow-moving ox wagons. Gaeser divided his troop up into four groups with Fredo, Ingamar and Scarila acting as leaders. Gaeser and the remaining companions formed the vanguard with the other troop sections riding to either side of the convoy and acting as a rearguard. The section leaders had licence to send out forage parties on a regular basis. Fodder for the horses and the oxen was a constant need. Two centuries of Alemanni marines marched in front of the convoy and another two marched at the rear. The Quadi soldiers and Pannonian militia drove the wagons and acted as wagon guards.

Each night Gaeser insisted that the wagons form a square and replicate a Roman marching fort as best they could. Four exits were to be left on each side of the square so that the cavalry could come and go. In the event of an attack during the day the wagons would form square with one century of marines on each side. Gaeser's troop would remain outside and intervene when he judged it necessary. I knew that my brother had the Battle of Adrianople in mind and wanted his cavalry to be able to make a surprise attack on the flanks of an enemy.

We set off hoping that, by the time we reached Mursa, Godigsel's relief column would not be too far away. We made timely progress on the Roman road. However, because the road followed the river, the route involved plenty of twists and turns. Gaeser was concerned that the road demanded that the wagons travel in single file. The road simply wasn't wide enough for two columns. It meant the convoy stretched for miles. If we had to form a defensive square it could not be achieved quickly if at all. Gaeser confessed to me that it was a weakness he had no answer for.

On the afternoon of the tenth day, we crossed the Drava River and entered the small town of Mursa and made camp. One of the Vandal sections came in to report the approach of around 150 Vandal tribesmen. They had been sent by Gunderic and were attempting to find us at Taurunum. They were

mostly youngsters who had foolishly followed
Radagarius into Italy. For the first time we heard
of the defeat of Radagarius' main force outside of
Florentia. When the other Goth armies heard the
news, they turned around and fled back across the
Alps. Gunderic had been ordered to shadow the
more easterly group as they crossed the Julian Alps
and followed the Drava River towards the Danube.
The Vandal element of the Goth group had
separated from the rest allowing Gunderic to make
contact. He warned the young Vandals that a Hun
army would eventually catch and destroy the main
band so that they had best break away and head for
Taurunum. The young Vandals pleaded for us to
allow them to join our convoy. They warned that
the main Goth band was only two days behind
them and that, though they were a disorganised
rabble, there were over twenty thousand of them.
We had little choice but to accept the young
Vandals. If we had to face overwhelming numbers
of Goths, then the extra fighting men could only
help.

As we travelled towards Municipium Sopianae
we sent Safrax and Tzason to scout for the main
Goth band. We believed the Goths would be
heading for the Arpad bridge believing that the
bridge was still controlled by their fellow
tribesmen. We had to push on in the hope that
Godigsel was approaching. Our two columns were
on a collision course. On the evening that we made

camp at Sopianae, Tzason rode in to tell us the Goth band was camped only ten miles away. Safrax was still watching them. We were already in a defensive square for the night so Gaeser made the simple decision to remain where we were and hope that the Goths would pass by the next day. The only problem with that was that we were next to the town and the Goths were desperate for food meaning that they might well come directly for us.

The next morning Gaeser sent out the four Vandal sections. He had split up the Vandal youngsters so that each section had an extra 40 or so riders. Gaeser allocated two sections to the north of the camp with orders to conceal themselves beyond the brim of a hill. We did likewise to the south. Hildiger was left to command the wagon fort. Safrax found us and said that the Goths were coming directly for the camp and the town. He thought the warriors numbered around 10,000 with the rest women and children. Around midday we finally saw them approach along the valley on both sides of a small stream. A few of the warriors at the front had horses but most were on foot. They looked like an unstoppable lava flow of humanity. Gaeser's plan of a surprise flank attack seemed unlikely to stop them with the numbers we had. We had our attention on the Goths as Gunderic and 470 troopers of the Vandal *ala* walked their horses up behind us.

Gaeser attempted to greet Gunderic with confidence.

"Good timing brother. We may have need of you."

"I like the plan Gaeseric. Unfortunately, the numbers don't work. You should have stayed in Taurunum like I told you."

"We have 400 Alemanni marines in the camp plus a few Quadi soldiers and the Pannonians of course. Over on the other ridge are another 90 Vandal cavalry."

"You are wrong brother. Over the ridge are 590 Vandal warriors. Our father is here. It is still going to be a close-run thing. Let's find out how keen our starving friends are to fight."

Gunderic took control. He ordered the troopers to form line on the top of the ridge so that they could be seen below. On the ridge across the valley a similar line formed. Gunderic ordered his troops to roar. We could hear a faint echo of the roar from across the valley. We walked our horses forward with our lances in the air. Godigsel's troops across the valley did likewise. The Goths stopped. The women and children at the rear began to run back the way they had come. The mounted Goth leaders tried to lead their men in an attack on our hill. Barely fifty followed them. The rest were streaming back after the women and children. When the leaders saw that they were isolated, they too turned and ran.

We stayed in camp for the rest of the day. Vandal troops kept watch on the movement of the Goths and reported that they had moved around the town to the north. Later in the afternoon two Vandal troops escorted a dispirited group of around 200 young Quadi towards the camp. We sent Fredo and his friends out to deal with them. The Quadi youngsters had all joined in with Radagarius for adventure, glory, and treasure. Now they begged for food and the opportunity to join us. We left Fredo to make the decision. He told them that they could march with the convoy on half rations as far as Lentia. There they had the option to cross back over the river to their homes where the Huns now ruled. Alternatively, if the youngsters could demonstrate Roman military discipline and follow orders, they might have the option to stay and travel with the Vandals. Each of Fredo's friends were given ten men to command so that we had two centuries of inexperienced Quadi soldiers to add to our forces.

The reunion between Godigsel and Flavia was a touching one. They had been apart for five years. After a period of reacquaintance in Flavia's wagon, the king of the Vandals joined us around the campfire, and we listened to Gunderic's account of the defeat of Radagarius. Gunderic's *ala* had been used as scouts throughout the campaign. In northern Italy they remained in the area around Patavium, as the eastern arm of Radagarius' forces had sacked the city. Octar had led the Hun army into the Po valley to link-up with Stilico. By the time Stilico had assembled sufficient forces to confront Radagarius' main army the Goths were besieging Florentia. At the battle of Fiesole on a hill outside Florentia Radagarius' forces had been destroyed. Octar's Hun and Saurus' Goths had won the battle for the Romans. The word was that 12,000 of Radagarius' best warriors had been conscripted into Stilico's Italian army. The number of slaves taken after the battle was so high that the bottom fell out of the slave market. Radagarius was executed in August. The last piece of Gunderic's news was the most disturbing. The third element of the Goth invasion force remained undefeated and, hearing the news of the battle of Fiesole, had turned back to recross the Alps. They had taken the Brenner pass and were following the Inn River north. They were heading for Raetia.

Godigsel related the progress of the Vandals in Raetia. They had spread out to the west of the Inn River. Augusta Vindelicum, the main city in northern Raetia, had been besieged. However the garrison showed no signs of surrendering. The Alans were spread across southern Raetia. Contact with the Alemanni to the west had not been positive and there had been skirmishes between rival bands. The news from the north was that although the Suebes were gathering near Castra Regina, the main Marcomanni army was in the north preventing the Burgundians from coming into their territory. To the dismay of Scarila, there was no news of the Siling Vandals.

Godigsel decided that the defeat of Radagarius gave Gunderic's *ala* sufficient reason, in the absence of any other orders, to return to their barracks. As the *ala's* barracks were now occupied by Huns, all agreed that Gunderic's men should join the convoy to Raetia.

The next day we set off once more with Godigsel frustrated at the slow pace of the oxen. At least with our combined armed forces of over 1,600 men we felt reasonably secure. Our food stocks were, however, rapidly diminishing. We managed to persuade Godigsel to rest for a day at the Flat Sea. It was a remarkable sight – an immense stretch of calm fresh water. We could fish, swim, wash and fill our water barrels. The north side of the lake had plentiful game. We were glad of the rest day because the next section of the journey led across countryside devastated by the passage of the Goths earlier in the year. It took us twenty days of hard travel with limited food stocks to reach Vindobona and the Danube River. The oxen looked the worse for wear and we needed to stop for another day by the river to let them, and the horses, graze in the water meadows. At Lentia, Fredo told all the Quadi boys who had joined us that they had behaved well during the long march. He gave them the choice of joining our migration under the command of Fredo and his friends or leaving to cross the river back to their home villages. Every one of them chose to stay with Fredo.

Ten days later we crossed the Inn River, and we re-joined the Vandal people. Godigsel said the empty fortress of Batavia, which had a small port, would make a good temporary home for Hildiger and the Alemanni marines. After a period of rest and recuperation Gunderic led his *ala* to Augusta Vindelicorum to see if the city was ready to surrender. Despite our relief at reaching our destination unscathed we were aware that the peace might soon be broken as another Goth army marched down the Inn River valley. With that in mind, Godigsel asked Gaeseric and the companions to travel south and find Respendial. If we could determine what the refugee Goths were intending so much the better.

Manius queried the recruitment of so many of Radagarius' warriors into the Roman army.

"Surely, master, taking so many enemy warriors into the Roman army was a dangerous practice."

It was dangerous but it was the only way Stilico could increase his forces. The senators of Rome and aristocracy of Italy refused to have the men working on their *latisfundia* conscripted into the army. When Radagarius invaded, Stilico had only 20,000 men in the army of Italy. He had to wait six months while the Goths pillaged northern Italy before he had enough reinforcements to give battle. Remember Saurus and the Greuthungi had been enemy warriors in 401 before changing sides. The army that defeated Radagarius were mainly Huns, Goths, and Alans.

Chapter 21

The return of the Goths

We rode south, with Safrax scouting ahead as usual. We each led a spare Alan horse and rode our barbs. The dogs bounded along happily at our side. The route was an easy one as we simply followed the river south. Our first encounter was with a convoy of Lacringi Vandals heading north led by Crixos. They reported that Goar's Alans had left their settlements and were moving west into Gaul. The Lacringi had not been invited to join with Goar's people and so were heading north to find the Vandals. Crixos had heard that a vast number of Goths were coming north and therefore they had decided to flee north and join up with Godigsel's Vandals. We questioned them on the whereabouts of Respendial's Alans. The Lacringi said they passed through some months ago heading west. They believed that they had settled to the north of Lacus Brigantius which the Alemanni called the Bodensee. We now had a decision to make. Strike west to find Respendial or carry on south and run into the Goths. Safrax returned from scouting and solved our dilemma. A Vandal *ala* was coming towards us along the riverbank. We rode on to greet Guntha and the Vandal troopers we had last seen five years before in 401.

Guntha's *ala* had ridden around the Goth masses. They had hoped to warn the Vandals of the Inn valley settlements of the Goths' approach. Guntha estimated that there were around 60,000 refugee Goths moving north to Raetia. Up to a third were women and children. Guntha's *ala* had ridden with Goar's Alans all through Alaric's invasion of Italy. Their original commander, General Abtin, had been killed at the battle of Polentia along with General Saul. Goar now commanded all the Alan troops as well as the Vandal *ala*. The Greuthungi Goth leader, Saurus, had been given command of all Roman forces in the west of Italy including 12,000 warriors recruited from Radagarius' forces. Stilico, for reasons unknown, had headed east after the battle of Fiesole and taken all the Hun forces with him. Guntha imagined some sort of campaign was planned for Illyricum, with Alaric's Trevingi expected to support Stilico.

Goar's command, which included Guntha's Vandal *ala,* had been ordered to shepherd the third and undefeated Goth force back across the Alps to Raetia. Guntha believed that Saurus had made a deal with the refugee Goths whereby they would be allowed to settle in Raetia in return for supplying a further 10,000 warriors for Saurus' army. Now that the Goths had arrived in southern Raetia, Goar had taken his Alan troops and all of his people from the Inn valley settlements and moved west into Gaul. He was following the orders of Stilico, and he had official passes for his people and the Alan forces to cross the Rhine at Argentorate. Apparently, there was a new usurper in Britannia and Stilico feared an invasion by the Britannia legions into Gaul. Goar's Alans were being sent by Stilico to block their path. Finally, Guntha explained that his Vandal *ala* had been ordered to monitor the Goths movements and ensure they settled in Raetia. They were then to follow Goar to the west. Guntha also held official passes to cross the bridge at Argentorate.

It was a lot of information to take in. Gaeser asked what the Romans planned for the Vandals. Guntha shrugged.

"I doubt the position of the Vandals was ever considered. The Romans think only to protect themselves. They do not know where the Vandals are. Even we did not expect to find you here. When we left there were only a few Vandals settled here. Are you saying that all the Asding Vandals have now migrated to the north of Raetia?"

Gaeser replied. "They have and all the northern Tisza valley Alans along with them, many thousands of them. The Huns control the Tisza valley. The Alans are somewhere to the west, and we have been sent to find them."

Guntha was at a loss as to what he should do. He, and most of his men, had family and friends amongst the Vandals and they been away for five years. When Guntha heard that Gunderic's *ala* had left the army and returned to join the Vandals in Raetia, he concluded that he should do the same. He said his men would also abandon the Roman army and come to help the Vandals fight the Goths. He concluded that, if the Vandals wanted to settle in Raetia, they were going to have to fight for every inch of land.

Gaeser was also unsure. "We are not certain what the Goths intend. We must find out. Perhaps we can reach some accommodation."

Traso offered a solution. "Coccas and I can infiltrate one of the Goth camps and find out their intentions."

At the same time Tzason and Safrax said they would ride west to find Respendial. We all nodded our agreement. We rode south for another two days and then made camp on a secluded forested hillside away from the river. Guntha explained that the Goth camps were impossible to miss and would be spread out over the next ten miles. Swapping to their Alan horses and borrowing some of Safrax's clothing Traso and Coccas trotted off to join the Goths. Tzason and Safrax rode their barbs west leading their spare Alan horses.

Two days later Traso and Coccas returned. They had managed to join one of the Goth bands as they camped. They were recognised as Trevingi from the way they spoke, but it had not mattered. There were other Trevingi Goths in the band who had escaped from slavery during the invasion. The various Goth tribes were all mixed up and there were other Germanic tribes there whom they did not recognise. The people were tired and hungry, and all believed that Raetia would be their salvation. The band leaders had been told that they would make Augusta Vindelicorum their main base. They believed the garrison, under orders from Mediolanum, would open the gates for them and then leave. All seemed to understand that the families would settle permanently in Raetia. The men accepted that they would have to fight for the Romans in due course. They did not foresee anyone contesting their presence in the province.

After another two days Tzason and Safrax returned. They reported that they had found an Alan patrol. Safrax had been recognised from the battle of Partiscum. The Alan warriors related that, after Respendial had heard of the crossing of Goar's Alans into Gaul, he had tried to follow suit. The Alemanni *foederati* had closed the bridge at Argentorate and refused to allow Respendial's Alans to cross the Rhine. Respendial had launched an attack, but the bridge had towers and a wall across the approaches and despite their overwhelming numbers the Alans had no way of overcoming the defences. The Alans had lost many warriors in the attempt. Respendial's people were on the move again following the Rhine north. They were committed to crossing into Gaul somewhere up-river.

Gaeser said that we should return to Godigsel with this news. Guntha was determined to come with us, but Gaeser asked him not to.

"Guntha, you and the *ala* have a pass to cross the Rhine. I suggest you use it. Once you are across, travel north. Follow the progress of Respendial's Alans on the other side. I believe the Vandals will also travel north and attempt to cross the Rhine at Mogontiacum. I know you and your men want to see your families again after such a long time, but you will be of more use to them on the other side of the river. There is the possibility that the Siling Vandals might join us at Mogontiacum. Together we may be strong enough to force a crossing. It seems Raetia is not to be our new home after all."

Back at Boiodorum, Godigsel was understandably upset with the news we reported. How was it that the invaders of Italy were to be rewarded with Raetia? It made no sense. Not only that, but Goar's people had been given free passage to Gaul. Stilico, of all people, had let the Vandals down. Gaeser had already predicted Godigsel's reaction to our news. So it came as no surprise when Godigsel explained his thoughts.

"We cannot fight the Goths for Raetia. We would lose too many. We must go north and hope to link up with the Silings. We must ask the Marcomanni for permission to travel through their territory. Gaeseric, you have met Hermeric. Can you and the companions go to Castra Regina and

243

negotiate our passage north? Have Fredo organise the Quadi to come with you. Take a little gift for Hermeric to smooth the negotiations."

Godigsel sent messengers to Gunderic at Augusta Vindelicorum, Hildiger at Batavia, and every Vandal community across the region. The message was to prepare to move north. He asked Scarila to travel north to find the Silings.

Gaeser and our remaining companions rode to Castra Regina accompanied by fifty mounted Quadi soldiers. We were welcomed into the same hall we had visited earlier in the year. Hermeric was not present and nor was his main army. The younger brother, Heremigarius, presided in his stead and seemed to delight in the power of his position. Some of the Marcomanni nobles seemed less pleased that they had to defer to the youngster. Both Fredo and Ingamar were able to translate the Marcomanni language if needed but Heremigarius insisted on Latin.

Hermeric was in the north making sure the Burgundians did not trouble the northern Marcomanni communities. Gaeser presented Heremigarius with a gold cloak clasp and asked for permission for the Asding Vandal people to progress north through Marcomanni land. Heremigarius made a great show of considering the request before finally giving permission. He encouraged us to follow the Neckar River north claiming that this would give us a safe route to Mogontiacum.

Heremigarius used a Latin term for the Rhine Franks we were unfamiliar with. He called them *Ripuarians*, which translated as river people, but I had never heard the term used before or since. He reassured us that, though there were Rhine Frank villages east of the Rhine, they would not interfere with our grand convoy. He warned us not to travel past the river Main in the north as it was beyond this river that the Rhine Franks lived in substantial numbers. They controlled the bridge and city at Mogontiacum, but their most important city was further up the river at Colonia. We enquired about the group we called the West Franks. Heremigarius called these people *Salians* and said that they lived much further up the Rhine where the river joined the Mare Germanicum.

When we asked if the Suebic federation would join us, Heremigarius was evasive. A large camp of Quadi and other Suebic tribes were camped on the north side of the river, but Heremigarius did not think they were ready to invade Gaul. They would wait for Hermeric to return and, even then, probably travel south towards the territory of the Alemanni before attempting to cross the river. Unless, of course, we forced a crossing ourselves.

By the time we had returned to Boiodorum, Gunderic was back from the siege of Augusta Vindelicorum. The siege was over, but it was not the Vandals who now controlled the city, it was the Goths. A large warband of Goths had arrived, and the Vandals had been forced to retreat. The city gates were thrown open and the garrison marched out to the west alongside a convoy of civilians. Had we needed any further encouragement to travel north, then Gunderic's report provided it.

Ingamar was concerned that his father and the older marines had become too settled in Castra Batavia and might not join the trek north. He asked us to join him in attempting to persuade Hildiger to join us. At the fortress we learnt that the Alemanni marines had four of their old ships in the section of the river above the Arpad bridge. We found that Hildiger had plans to raid south of the bridge and retrieve more of his former ships. He was sorry to hear that the Vandals would be going north but was quite clear that he and his senior men did not want to leave the secure fortress they now possessed. Vangio explained that the families of the marines had found the journey across Pannonia a difficult one. They did not want to repeat the experience. He was open, however, to the younger marines, who had no families, following Ingamar.

Vangio assembled the marines in the fortress that day and informed them of the choices they all faced. He stated clearly that there were too many marines for the ships they now possessed and that, if any of the single marines wanted to leave with his son and the Vandals, they may do so. Ingamar gave an impassioned speech about the adventures and riches that awaited them in a defenceless Gaul if only they had the courage to grab the opportunity. Vangio called for a vote knowing already that the majority would stay with him in Castra Batavia. Nevertheless, seventy young marines elected to follow Ingamar and leave the fortress.

We had not been part of the main Asding Vandal migration from the Tisza valley to Raetia. So, when we came to ride along the entire length of the Vandal convoy of wagons, the numbers overwhelmed us. The wagons stretched for over ten miles. Of course, they were not all Asding Vandals. We had Pannonians, Quadi, Alemanni and the Lacringi Vandals in our migrating band. We had caught a glimpse of the river of Goth humanity flowing north up the Inn River valley and could only conclude that our stream of multiple wagon trains was just as large.

Yannus asked, "did Godigsel ever attempt to count all the people?"

He did not. When Gaeseric had become king, he made a point of holding a census. However, that was much later.

Chapter 22

Confrontations with the Rhine Franks

The valley of the Neckar River was a good route to follow initially. It took us through Marcomanni territory along a Roman road in the northerly direction we wished to follow. Our migrating group, whilst being as large as the refugee Goth column we had witnessed, was much better organised. We had far more horses, wagons, animals, supplies and discipline. Godigsel gave strict orders that the Marcomanni villages were not to be attacked. He would organise payment for any food and fodder the villages had to sell. Godigsel used his, and Gunderic's, experience of commanding a Roman *ala* to form the Vandal warriors into twenty mounted squadrons of 500. He followed Roman cavalry organisation and appointed decurions to command troops of thirty warriors. The troops provided a constant screen to the left, right and rear of the convoys. Gunderic and his *ala* had command of the vanguard. Godigsel and his oathsworn rode in the middle of the convoy. Gaeser and the companions supported by 50 mounted Quadi soldiers rode at the rear of the huge column behind 70 marching Alemanni marines. The Quadi foot soldiers marched at the head of the column. The Pannonian militia and the

Vandal villagers drove the wagons. Our route of march north ran some forty miles from the Rhine to our west and about 10 miles away from the old Germania Roman *limes* to the east. The Lautertal *limes*, as they were known, had been abandoned a long time before.

When the river turned west and headed directly for the Rhine, we sent our scouts out to search for alternative routes. We calculated we were less than 100 miles from our destination, the area opposite the bridge at Mogontiacum. The Neckar River joined the Rhine between two major Roman cities, Borbetomagus and Noviomagus. We believed Rhine Frank *foederati* garrisoned both those cities although we would later find out that they were actually manned by Alemanni *foederati*. The scouts found that the people in the villages they passed through now hid from them unlike in the Marcomanni villages. We presumed that the river route would take us into Rhine Frank territory.

The road directly north was little more than a track but did have the benefit of passing a string of small abandoned auxiliary forts which had once formed the frontier before the Lauteral *limes* were built. Gaeser advised that we should follow the route directly north and use the forts to provide temporary camps. The scouts had not found any people in the area, suggesting it was a neutral ground between the Marcomanni and the Franks.

Gaeser had a feeling that Heremigarius' advice about the Rhine Franks could not be relied upon.

Godigsel did not listen. He took the decision to follow the river to the west as far as the town of Heidelberg where a good Roman road turned to the north. For Godigsel the quality of the roads and the difficulty of the terrain on the northern route were the crucial factors. He felt secure with an army of over 12,000 to protect the convoy. It was a decision we all came to regret.

The attack, when it came, hit the convoy behind the vanguard and it came from both sides. The low hills were heavily forested, and the flanking Vandal troops simply did not see the Rhine Franks until they were only a few hundred yards away. The cavalry quickly lost their advantage when Frank warriors swarmed all over them. The Rhine Frank warriors hacked horse and man down with huge double-handed axes.

We were several miles away at the rear of the column, and by the time we arrived, Godigsel had managed to stabilise the situation. Wagons had been turned to form a rough defensive barrier on both sides and the Quadi foot soldiers were holding their own along the wagon line. Godigsel's oathsworn were carving a path through the main body of Franks at the front. When Gunderic's *ala* charged into the back of the Franks, they broke and ran for the trees.

The Rhine Franks were ferocious fighters and employed a weapon we had not seen before. The francisca is a throwing axe and the Franks used them to deadly effect. The Vandal troops caught in the attack suffered badly and hundreds were killed. The vulnerability of the convoy when travelling in line in enemy territory was obvious. Our army was too spread-out to provide protection at every point.

Godigsel made the obvious decision to travel back the way we had come and follow the route north past all the abandoned forts. Gaeser and the companions now led the way and Gunderic formed the rearguard, ensuring the Franks did not follow us. The progress of the convoy slowed considerably. Over some sections we had to double team the wagons to get them over hilly sections. Gaeser devised a plan whereby each fort that was not too dilapidated was garrisoned by foot soldiers. The lookout towers in the fort had been built to provide early warning of attack. The forest would have been cleared for a mile on either side in the days when it was the frontier. Now the forest had regrown. Nevertheless, the towers still provided good views of the surrounding area. The convoy camped in between forts and the garrison only left when the entire convoy had passed. Cavalry troops escorted the infantry garrisons forward from one fort to another. One of the benefits of passing through this wooded hilly area where few people lived was that there was plenty of game to be hunted. Safrax hunted with the dogs every day. The companions' campfire was always well served with meat.

Small bands of Franks were seen following our progress north. We doubled our troops on the western side to deter them. Every now and then small bands of warriors would burst between troops and attack a wagon. They grabbed what they could and ran. The constant threat was demoralising, but there was little we could do to prevent it. The Franks seemed to disappear into the forests. We knew that they were there, but we could not find them.

Eventually we came to the end of the line of forts and the forested hills. The scouts reported a major river away to the northeast and an abandoned Roman town and possible former legionary fortress to the northwest. The bridge at Mogontiacum was only twenty miles away. The morale of the convoy was low, and our food stocks were dwindling. We all feared that the Rhine Franks would launch a major attack. Godigsel decided to fortify the abandoned town found by the scouts and wait there for the Siling Vandals to arrive. He sent an embassy to the Marcomanni with gold to buy food.

The town or fortress had been built in a wooden square. A small stream ran by the side giving a good supply of water. The west and east walls were largely still intact. Some parts of the north wall still stood as did several buildings in the centre. The south side had no remaining wall at all. Godigsel ordered as many of the wagons into the town as possible. The remainder formed a double line barrier to the south. The Quadi and Alemanni soldiers and marines were ordered to man the southern wagon barriers to the town. A workforce was organised to rebuild the northern defences by piling up old timbers and stones and digging a defensive ditch. The western gate still had a standing watch tower. As the town sat in an open plain, we would have early warning of any attack.

Several elderly Frank tribesmen, too old to flee, lived in a section of the town. Godigsel ordered that they were not to be harmed. The locals called the settlement Dieburg which Ingamar said simply meant the castle. In the biggest building we found an inscription giving the Roman name of Vicus Vetus Ulpius and a date from the time of the emperor Trajan. We also found an underground Mithraeum with a sculpture of the god killing a bull. The worship of Mithras had been extremely popular within the Roman army before Christianity became accepted. Flavia and Godigsel set up a court of sorts in the main building and most senior Vandal nobles and their families joined them there.

In the next two weeks Gaeser led the companions on a long scouting mission. By riding our barb horses, we felt we could outrun any who might come after us. We rode to the Rhine and followed the river up to Mogontiacum. The Rhine *classis* had a river port about ten miles south of the city and it was on the eastern bank of the river and so was of interest to us. We sent Ingamar and Kitan down to the port hoping that the marines were Alemanni. We saw ferries operating across the river. Small groups could cross at this point quite easily and without the knowledge of the city garrison. Ingamar returned and confirmed that the marines were indeed Alemanni.

"They are sailing up to Mongontiacum. They do not go any further than that anymore. They say the Rhine Franks are becoming increasingly hostile to them. There is no love lost between the Alemanni and the Rhine Franks. For some consideration they would happily transport a small group across the river. The *ripenses* say they passed an endless convoy of Alan horsemen and wagons heading this way. The Alans were opposite Noviomagus when the *laburnum* sailed past."

The defensive works protecting the crossing at Mogontiacum were more substantial than we had anticipated. We could not get near to the city; however even from a distance we could see that the walls were high with many tower forts along the sides and on both sides of the main gates. The Pons Ingeniosa was a stone pillar bridge with enough width to take two directional traffic. On the eastern bank a stone castle, Castellum Mattiacorum, protected the approaches to the bridge. We imagined that this was the castle that prevented the Burgundians from crossing. A further problem was that the bridge was on the north bank of the river Main. The bridge over the Main River was a much simpler wooden affair and was unguarded. We knew we could easily capture this bridge, but our convoy would, nevertheless, be vulnerable crossing the river Main. We continued our journey by following the Main east and then eventually south. As we did so we realised that the river our scouts had reported to the east was, in fact, the Main looping south. If Heremigarius was correct that substantial numbers of Rhine Franks lived beyond the river Main, then we had managed to place ourselves in a situation where we had Franks to the north, east and west of us.

We reported our findings to Godigsel and Gunderic. They, in turn, told us that there was no news from the Silings. Of more immediate concern was the lack of response from the Marcomanni. Our food was running out. We considered the option of attempting to take the bridge and force a crossing without the Silings. None of us felt comfortable about taking that option. We all believed that the Rhine Franks, who watched us from afar, would attack before we even reached the river Main bridge. Godigsel decided that Gunderic should lead several *alae* towards the Rhine on a raiding mission. The Franks were our enemies, and we set out to destroy their villages on the eastern side of the Rhine, steal their food and drive their warriors further south. It was to be revenge for our losses at the skirmish at Heidelberg.

The raids were successful and brutal. Any villagers that were caught were slaughtered and the village huts were burned. Gunderic brought back wagons full of grain, fodder, and slaughtered pigs. We would not starve for the time being. On the other hand it became inevitable that the Rhine Franks would respond and come against us. Godigsel was confident we could defend the position we had and the plains around it. It was another question as to how long we could stay where we were. Our food stocks would not last long and we were still faced with the fundamental problem of how to cross the river. Our lookouts in the old tower searched the skyline for signs of the Siling Vandals to the east and the Alans to the west.

⊕

Manius wanted some clarification on the *Ripuarian* Franks.

"Master, I am aware that King Childeric and the Franks rule much of northern Gaul, but I have never heard of any other Franks. What happened to the Rhine Franks?"

It seems likely that they were defeated by the West Franks, and subsequently joined with them.

The Franks we know today are a combination of the two groups, many other minor tribes plus the Gallo-Roman population of northern Gaul.

Chapter 23

Before the battle of Mogontiacum

There was little doubt in our minds that the raids on the Rhine Frank villages would trigger a response. None spoke of the danger, though Godigsel appeared resigned to another battle. He felt confident that, if the Franks advanced across the open plain, then his cavalry strength would prevail. If the cavalry failed to stop the attack, then the defences we had built would hold them off.

Two weeks after the raids the Rhine Franks began to assemble in considerable numbers to the west of the town. We estimated that there might be up to 5,000 warriors. After a day of doing nothing, they began to move to the south as if in preparation for an attack on the wagon barriers we had placed to the south side of the town. We prepared to make a mass cavalry attack on the Franks as soon as they broke the cover of the trees to the south. Gunderic would lead our forces out of the east gate and Godigsel would exit out of the western gate. Gaeser was told to organise the wagon barrier defences. The women, children and animals were moved to the centre of the town. Our focus was entirely on the south and the west when the lookouts cried out pointing in the opposite direction.

A massive army had appeared to the north. They looked to number at least twice as many as the Franks to the south. We had little doubt that the Rhine Franks to the north and east had crossed the river Main without our knowledge. Godigsel called an emergency council. The balance of the opposing forces had changed, and we were now almost certainly outnumbered. We were also surrounded and trapped in the town. We would need help and Godigsel looked to the companions to search for it. He asked for volunteers to ride out to find any friendly forces that might come to our aid. With our superior horses and leading spare Alan mounts we would not be caught.

Tzason spoke first. "I will ride south and seek Respendial and the Alans. If the Alans had continued north, then they should not be too far away."

Safrax was quick to support him. "I will go with Tzason."

Gaeser had other ideas. "No Safrax, let Skara accompany Tzason. You are our best scout and tracker. We need you to find Scarila and the Silings."

The Silings had been expected for the last few weeks and none could understand why there had been no word. Wherever they were, they could not be far away. Safrax agreed to go and search for them. He preferred to go alone.

Ingamar was next to volunteer. "Kitan and I will go to the Marcomanni. We will attempt to bring back Hermeric's mounted army."

Only a mounted force could possibly intervene in time. The messengers left immediately. Godigsel moved on to the deployment of his forces. Cavalry was our strength, and we had to use it. Gunderic was given overall command of the cavalry. He would take the main force of eight alae and attack the northern Frank army from the west. Gaeser seemed not to react at all when his father gave him command of two alae and told him to harass the northern army through the eastern gate. Two senior decurions were each to lead two alae and instructed to attack the Franks' southern army from both sides. Godigsel allocated 2,000 Vandal warriors to the southern boundary along with all the Quadi soldiers. He put Fredo in command of the southern defensive line of wagon barriers. The Alemanni marines and the Pannonians were to man the east and west walls. Godigsel would take his oathsworn and two thousand five hundred men to the northern defences and fight on foot.

Flavia's organisation of the women and children highlighted the seriousness of the situation. She had a square of wagons drawn up around the central buildings and encouraged the womenfolk to arm themselves. Teams of boys were delegated to fill all available water skins and be ready to relay them to the warriors on the front line. Older boys were to use their bows and slings over the heads of the defenders. Flavia acquired a helmet and spear and stood on top of a wagon giving instructions to the people she had adopted.

She called out as I rode by.

"Be strong Marcus and watch your brother's back."

Our old tutor, Gregor, was forever at Flavia's side. He shook a fist of determination and called out.

"Don't worry Marcus I will protect your mother if she needs protecting. I think she believes she is a reincarnation of Boudicca."

Diomedes had taught us of Boudicca, the warrior Queen of the Iceni tribe in Britannia, who had led a rebellion against the Romans. The image of Boudicca I had in my mind, influenced my lasting memory of my mother. I will always remember her as a warrior Queen of the Vandals rather than as a Roman lady.

As dusk descended, we saw the campfires of the two armies of Franks fill the horizon to both north and south. We had an evening to prepare for battle. Godigsel set watches on every wall but our experience with the Franks suggested a night attack was unlikely. Warriors spent time with their families and friends in quiet contemplation. Women exhorted their men to fight bravely but come back whole. Fathers told young sons to protect their mothers and siblings. The seven remaining companions sat together, and we recalled the many adventures of our young lives, the day at the hippodrome, the day we rode into Radagarius' camp, the day we stood behind the front line at Partiscum.

We all knew that the next day would be vastly different. Gaeser would lead 1,000 men in an assault on a vast army of Franks. They would include his own troop equipped with the extra-long lances. We would do well to survive. Axxa was annoyed that both Kitan and Skara were absent. He said that he would fight on Gaeser's right, his non-shield side. Traso asked to take the left side of Gaeser with Wada left of him. Coccas would be to Axxa's right with Ulli next to him. My position was never questioned. I was Scuta. I always watched Gaeser's back. I would hold my long lance aloft and fill any gap that appeared.

Gaeser bade me follow him as he went around the men of the *alae* he would be leading. He asked the names of those he did not know and took interest in their families. Gaeser was just seventeen years old, yet the men accepted him openly as their leader. He spoke well and was well liked. I got the feeling that men would follow him and, what is more, fight for him. He had a clear idea of the battle tactics he wanted to employ the next day and the troopers all listened carefully. We had seen at the Heidelberg skirmish how River Frank warriors, even though on foot, had engulfed our troopers, killing both horses and men. Gaeser emphasised that he wanted the first two strikes on the flanks of the Franks to be with javelins. After throwing our javelins we would turn and break away before we could be caught up in hand-to-hand fighting. Gaeser gave the example of the Alan charges at Partiscum and how effective they were. Each trooper carried two javelins so we could make two charges before engaging for a final impact. Gaeser hoped that his own troop could make an impact with our long lances and the companions more so with our bigger horses.

Those that could, slept a few hours, but many did not. I did eventually close my eyes listening to Gaeser relate the stories of the Spartans before the Battle of Thermopylae. I dreamed of waxing my hair and polishing my bronze shield. My mother spoke to me in the dream telling me to "come home with your shield or on it." At that point I woke with a start to hear a strange humming drone coming from the north. Godigsel rode around every corner of the town explaining the sound to his warriors so that none would fear it. Some Germanic tribes employed the *baritus*, a strange and haunting sound when sung by thousands. It was supposed to put fear into enemies and inspire bravery amongst their own. The Roman general Varus had lost some 15,000 men in the forests of Germania four hundred years earlier. The few survivors from the three Roman legions lost in the Teutoburger Wald disaster told of how they had been terrified by the Germanic *baritus*. Many different Germanic tribes had combined to defeat the Romans back then. Nowadays the Chatti, the Cherusci, the Marsi and the Bructeri were simply referred to as Franks. The Teutoburger Forest was only one hundred miles north of where we were.

Fortunately, we had an open plain to do battle on. It was cavalry country. Gaeser went to consult with his father and brother. The Vandal warriors looked nervous and Gaeser wanted to reverse the situation and make the Franks fearful of us. He explained that the Franks had observed us for several weeks. Gaeser sensed that they were reluctant to attack across the open plain for fear of the Vandal cavalry. The Rhine Franks who had crossed the river Main from the north and east, however, had little knowledge of the Vandals or how we fought. He wanted us to display the full might of the Vandal cavalry to the northern Frank army and see if that had an effect. Godigsel agreed with the plan.

Gunderic took 5,000 mounted Vandal warriors out of the western gate as Gaeser led 2,000 out of the eastern gate. We formed a line two deep across from either side of the northern defences with Gunderic's greater numbers curving around to the north. It was an awe-inspiring sight and sound for we all roared our war cry in unison. The northern Frank army made no response. The southern Frank army, however, did. The lookouts in the tower pointed to the south. The southern Franks were streaming across the open plain towards the wagon barriers where Fredo commanded. The battle of Mogontiacum had begun and it was a battle that nearly ended the very existence of the Asding Vandals.

Yannus asked, "How did you feel that morning knowing that you faced a full-scale battle for the first time with the possibility of being killed?"

I was physically sick. I could not eat. I felt terrified. I think everyone did, but most tried not to show it. I was terrified of being killed or wounded but I was also terrified of letting Gaeser down.

Chapter 24

The Battle of Mogontiacum

It was early December in 406. The attack of the Rhine Franks on the southern side of the town was the signal for all hell to be let loose. The next two hours were a complete blur of action and danger. Gaeser sent two *alae* south to attack the southern Franks as Godigsel had planned. Gunderic did likewise on the western side. As soon as the northern Franks observed an element of our forces turning away they themselves advanced. The leaders of the northern Frank army were mounted but chose to fight on foot. They formed a huge V shaped wedge and headed directly for Godigsel and the northern defences. The warriors moved surprisingly quickly, jogging across the open ground. Gunderic was the first to respond sending his men into a massive flank attack on the side of the advancing northern Franks. The body of the wedge moved to the west to engage with the Vandal cavalry. The head of the wedge continued towards the northern defences and Godigsel. The moment had come, and we charged in line. Our attack stopped twenty metres from the side of the advancing Franks, and we hurled our javelins with all our strength. We turned right in unison to ensure we did not get caught up in close combat. Our barb horses were superb fighting animals, but it was noticeable that the Alan horses could turn more quickly.

We retreated to a small hill fifty metres away and reassembled. We had a thousand troopers in our line and, although I could not be certain, I could not see any empty saddles. We charged again but this time the Franks were ready with a reception. Francisca axes, spears and arrows greeted us as we threw our last javelins. When we regrouped again there were several empty saddles. Despite our attacks the main body of the Franks seemed undiminished on our side. On the other side Gunderic's forces were having a major impact. As far as we could see, there was a chaotic hand-to-hand struggle between the two forces. The leaders and the front section of the northern Frank wedge were not involved with Gunderic's forces and were now directly engaged with Godigsel's warriors on the northern defences. There were effectively two separate battles and neither appeared to be going well for the Vandals. Gaeser's tactics of hit and run were not having enough of an impact.

He called the decurions to his side and said we would form a wedge, head directly for Godigsel, and fight our way through. Gaeser's troop, with their long lances, would be the tip of the wedge with the companions and their barb horses at the centre. Before Gaeser could order the charge, a familiar voice called out from behind us.

"Prince Gaeseric, wait for us and we will join you."

Scarila and a small group of young Siling warriors rode up beside us. Gaeser gestured with his hands as he asked the question on all of our minds.

"Is this all you have with you? Where is Safrax? Where is Fredbal and the rest of the Silings?"

Scarila pointed behind him.

"Fear not. Safrax found us. He rides with King Fredbal and the Siling Nobles."

Hollering and whooping one thousand Siling nobles appeared on the horizon and charged into the Franks as if on an auroch hunt. Scarila continued pointing to the far side of the battle.

"Over there, Prince Gaeseric, I think those are Alans attacking on the other side."

True enough, huge waves of Alan warriors were riding into the western flank of the Franks allowing Gunderic's men to disengage and reform. More Alans could be seen circling around the back of the Franks. The Alan attacks were unceasing and deadly. The front section of the northern Frank army was however overcoming Godigsel's warriors and entering the town.

There was no time to lose and no choice but to engage with the enemy. We charged to save our king and his oathsworn, with Gaeser and the companions the spearhead in our wedge formation. As soon as we struck the Franks with our long lances, the effectiveness of the weapon used from the height of our horses was clear. We repeatedly punched forward with the lances preventing the Franks from getting within striking range. When Gaeser's lance snapped in two, Flamma reared up on his hind legs and smashed his hooves down on the nearest Frank. The other barbs followed suit as they barged into the enemy forcing us forward. Franks attempted to creep under the rearing Flamma and stab into his underbelly, but they only met the fangs of Wolf and Shirkar. The dogs, forever at Flamma's side, were a continuous frenzy of biting, tearing, and snarling. The problem was that we advanced much further than the other troops. Franks folded around our sides as we pushed forwards. The fighting became intense, and men started to die all around us.

Gaeser should have died that day. He did not because others died to protect him. Axxa repeatedly leaned across with his shield to stop spears driving towards my brother as he exposed his body with a sword stroke. I retained my lance and drove it forward over Gaeser's head time after time. Traso fought with incredible ferocity to clear a path on Gaeser's left. Coccas saved Axxa's life when he blocked an axe about to take Axxa's head. It cost him his life as a spear was thrust into his unprotected right side. Ulli was fully engaged fighting for his life and could do nothing to protect his partner. I pushed my barb forward to take Coccas' place in the line. Traso's barb was hacked down by a giant Frank with a two-handed axe. Traso fell backwards and did not witness his twin's demise. Traso was not quick to recover from his fall and the axeman would have ended his life had not Wada barged his horse into the big man. Turning his horse to protect Traso left Wada's back exposed, and a thrown spear struck him between his shoulders. Scarila and two of his Siling friends arrived a moment too late to save Wada, but they did save Traso. It took all three of them to strike the giant down. The giant's death gave our attack momentum, and we edged forward slowly. The Franks were now stepping backwards and increasingly to the north. Our progress forward encountered less resistance.

We had a moment's breathing space. We looked up to see Gunderic and his men fighting towards us from the other side. If we could battle through to meet each other then we could cut the head of the northern Frank army from its body. Our wedge formation split the Franks before us into two. Those to our right retreated north attempting to avoid the Siling nobles and the Alans. Those to our left ran towards the northern defences. We could see no sign of Godigsel and his warriors. The head of the northern Frank army had taken the northern defences and entered the town.

We fought through to meet with Gunderic's forces in front of the northern defences. I looked around and made a rough guess that of Gaeser's 1,000 warriors we must have lost around 200 men. The shock of the extent of our own casualties paled when we saw how few were with Gunderic. Gaeser asked Gunderic bluntly where his men were. Gunderic answered aggressively.

"This is all that remain. The fighting was savage. They hacked down our horses and many died. We would all have perished had not Tzason arrived when he did. But this is not over. We must find our father. The Franks are inside the town."

There were so many dead and wounded on the northern defensive line, both Vandal and Frank, that we could not pass with our horses. The defensive ditch we had dug had been filled with bodies. We dismounted and worked our way across. In the centre of the line, we found our father's oathsworn dead in a ring around Godigsel. We knew it was our father from his position, his clothes, and his helmet. Underneath his shield I found the richly decorated Roman sword and scabbard gifted to the Vandal king by Alaric. Godigsel's body and face were so mutilated as to be unrecognisable.

From the top of the northern defences, we could see the Franks swarming over the inner wagon square around the central building. The Vandal women were on the wagons determined to protect their children. Pannonian militia and Alemanni marines were running from the east and west walls to help them. We ran as fast as we could to join the fight. I saw Gregor fighting for all he was worth to protect his mistress. Flavia stood tall on top of the central wagon thrusting with her spear. In seconds Gregor was swept aside by an axe blow and our mother struck down by a sword. Those women that lived ran back to the building chased by the Frank warriors.

We reached the line of wagons where the women had fought and viewed the carnage. Every one of us had lost someone dear to us. We stopped and regrouped. The central building was surrounded. Fredo had marched a century of soldiers up from the southern barriers. It told us the battle at the south was over. We estimated that there were several hundred Franks in the large building along with all the Vandal women and children who had sheltered there.

Before we could decide what to do, a long-haired Frank chieftain stepped out holding a young Vandal boy by the hair.

"Give us free passage to the north or else we will slaughter your women and children," he demanded in the Frankish language.

His words were not entirely clear to us, but their intent was. Gunderic roared back.

"Touch one hair on their heads and you will all die painful deaths, Frank."

Again, the message got across even if the exact words were not understood. Fredo appeared by our side. Gaeser stepped forward pulling Fredo along to translate for him.

"Frank, the battle is over, and you have lost. Throw down your weapons. We give you free passage north. Go and tend to your dead and do not trouble us anymore. You have my word we will not harm you. Take the eastern gate for the northern gate is blocked with the dead."

The Franks threw down their weapons as they trudged out of the building. The surrounding crowd pulled back to open a path to the east gate. Immediately there were hisses and insults from the crowds on either side. Stones were thrown, but it was when a young Vandal woman stepped up, spear in hand, that the hostile atmosphere turned truly violent. She cried out as she slammed the spear into the back of the rearmost Frank.

"This is for my man."

All eyes turned to Gaeser including mine. He remained impassive and showed no reaction. Whether he meant it as a signal, I will never know. The Vandal women took his silence as permission and assaulted the defenceless Franks with whatever weapons were at hand. When the Franks turned to protect themselves and fend off the attacks from the women, the Vandal men stepped in to spear the Franks. Within a few minutes every

Frank warrior was dead and, in several cases, mutilated.

It was over. The history scrolls record that the Vandals defeated the Franks at a battle near the city of Mogontiacum but lost their king in the process. The history scrolls are wrong. The battle of Mogontiacum was effectively a series of battles and the Asding Vandals did not win. Gunderic's struggle with the Franks was going badly until the Alans intervened. He lost most of his men in the fight. Godigsel was defeated on the northern defences of the town. Godigsel and all 2,500 of his men died there. There was no evidence of any form of retreat. The southern defences held the Rhine Franks at the barriers with the aid of the Vandal *alae* attacking from the sides. They suffered heavy losses and the Franks had only retreated when Respendial's Alans had arrived. It was a victory of sorts. All acknowledged Fredo as an inspirational leader. The action on the eastern side where we were was not pivotal to the outcome. We contributed to the battle as did the Siling nobles, but we did not decide it. The Alans won the battle of Mogontiacum. The Franks lost the battle and suffered huge losses. The Asding Vandals lost their king and over half their warriors but survived as a people albeit a severely diminished one.

The Vandal families walked out to the scenes of the fighting to find the bodies of their loved ones. We were no different. We found our mother and laid her out on her wagon. We placed Gregor's body at her feet along with Flavia's two assistants. Gunderic brought Godigsel's body and laid it next to Flavia. Tzason rode in at that point, with Safrax, asking for news of his family. We left the dead to search for what we hoped were the living. Safrax knew where we would find them. He walked into the horse herd and came out with Tzason's mother, sister Farah and the other Alan youngsters. Tzason's family and their young friends had hidden amongst the horses when the Franks had broken into the town. Safrax hugged Tzason's mother whilst Tzason hugged his sister. Farah quickly broke away and ran into the arms of Skara, revealing a relationship we had previously been unaware of.

Whilst there was rejoicing for some, most grieved for their losses. It was too late in the day to deal with the dead. Those with the skills attended to the wounded in the central building. Gunderic ordered the food stocks to be used and animals to be slaughtered. Fires were built in every section of the town to cook the food. We were aware that a vast tented city had appeared to the west as the Alans camped for the night. The Siling nobles rode away to the east to join the main Siling wagon convoy that was slowly coming towards us. Warriors slumped to the ground and accepted food from the women. Those women who had lost their men befriended the warriors without a woman. A lot of new relationships were formed that night with many of the young Quadi soldiers and Alemanni marines acquiring new Vandal partners and, in some cases, new Vandal families.

Manius asked, "Was that the point when all the different tribes began to merge into a new people?"

I think it was. After that day, the western Germanic tribes of the Alemanni, the Marcomanni and the Quadi were simply referred to as Suebes. The Asdings mixed freely with the Silings and accepted Alans, Suebes, Pannonians, Gallo-Romans, and slaves into their own migrating group. Bands of Goths would join us later. By the time we reached Africa you could say that we had become an entirely new people. Nevertheless, the Romans still called us Vandals.

Chapter 25

After the Battle of Mogontiacum

The morning after the battle we were greeted by a grim sight. Flocks of crows and other birds had descended onto the battlefield and rats appeared out of nowhere. All were feasting on the mounds of dead bodies. Hundreds of horses wandered around searching for grass. Safrax, Farah and the Alan youngsters rode out to collect as many horses as they could. The younger members from Respendial's camp were out on the plain with the same intentions. The Alan youngsters used their lassos to haul in the stray horses and tie them together. Gunderic sent out Vandal riders to help Safrax retain as many of our horses as possible. Respendial's Alans took most, and none could begrudge them their reward. Alan women in their hundreds worked their way through the northern battlefield with grim determination, stripping the dead of anything of value. The Vandal women did likewise on those that had fallen at the northern defences and elsewhere. The dead would soon become a problem but before we could deal with that, we had a fallen king to mourn.

Gunderic decided to make a funeral pyre for Godigsel, Flavia and their servants in the centre of the town. As we now had a surplus of wagons, he decided to use Flavia's wagon as the centre of the pyre. Gaeser went to strip the wagon of its valuable contents. Gunderic was aware of the treasure contained in the old Roman pay chest, and had it transferred to his own wagon. I was amazed to find another treasure in my mother's wagon. It was my father's, my real father's, military uniform, armour, sword, and helmet. He had been a *pretorian prefectus* and the sculptured breast plate was magnificent. The ornate sword and plumed helmet were worthy of any Roman general. When the pyre was ready Gunderic wasted no time on ceremony. We had thousands to burn not least two of Gaeser's companions. The people gathered round the fire to acknowledge their king and his Roman woman. After a suitable period of silence, as the pyre began to subside, the first of the chants began.

"GUN-DER-RIC, GUN-DER-RIC, GUN-DER-RIC."

Quite a few eyes turned to Gaeser to see his reaction. Gaeser showed no hesitation. He cried out.

"All hail, Gunderic, King of the Asdings."

Every voice there joined in. There were none to challenge him. Virtually every senior member of the Asding royal family had died along with Godigsel. I presented Godigsel's sword and scabbard to the new king. Gunderic was just 27 years old.

Gunderic's first command was for the Vandal dead to be gathered and burnt. Many of the Vandals were Arian Christians and would have preferred a Christian burial for their loved ones. Certainly, our mother would have been horrified by the prospect of being burnt on a pyre. However, burial was not a practical option. Ulfred, our military chaplain had died fighting alongside Godigsel, and, in any case, there were simply too many bodies. As it was, we would leave all the Frank dead to rot.

Gaeser and the companions made a separate pyre for Coccas and Wada. We all donned our blue cloaks and sat on our barb horses while we paid tribute to our lost friends. Safrax and Scarila both attended. To brighten our mood and acknowledge the bravery he had displayed during the battle, Gaeser asked Scarila to join the companions. Despite the sad occasion there was no hiding Scarila's delight. Without the slightest hesitation Scarila swore the companions' oath. Gaeser presented Scarila with Coccas' blue cloak and his Vandal cross shield. Safrax led up Coccas' barb horse which had survived the battle. Traso's barb had died when it was struck down by the Frank giant, but he now had Wada's horse. Ulli formally asked for Traso's forgiveness for not preventing Coccas' death. None blamed Ulli least of all Traso who insisted Ulli replace Wada as his riding partner. Gaeser asked Safrax if he wished to be a companion, but he declined. He would scout for us whenever we needed but wanted to spend his time with Tzason's mother and his horses. So, we were seven companions with, now, five remaining Vandal guard companions, or we would be if Ingamar and Kitan returned.

Fredo requested that all his Quadi soldiers be allowed to have a horse. We had so many surplus horses that it made perfect sense. Of course, the Pannonians and Alemanni marines were included. Gaeser suggested that every warrior should have a second horse so that we could travel as fast as the Alans did.

Ingamar and Kitan returned the next day along with Hermeric and an advance guard of the Marcomanni army from the north. Hermeric was gracious in his condolences on the death of Godigsel and congratulations on the election of Gunderic as king. He apologised for the absence of Marcomanni support in the battle. Hermeric explained that he had left instructions for his younger brother, Heremigarius, to support the Vandals and bring them food. Neither, of course, had happened, and we could see that Ingamar had a story to tell.

While Gunderic and Hermeric went into a long conference, we took Ingamar aside to hear what had happened. When Ingamar and Kitan had found the Marcomanni outside of Castra Regina, the nobles had been assembled in anticipation of action to support the Vandals. Heremigarius had received the gold Godigsel had sent to procure food, but he had simply kept it. When Ingamar demanded the Marcomanni nobles ride to support the Vandals, Heremigarius made a great show of being in command and overruled his nobles. The nobles all wanted to help but Heremigarius refused to let them. He said that it was too late and that the battle would be over by the time they arrived. Ingamar was incandescent with rage that he had failed to bring help and that he had missed the battle.

Later that day a convoy of wagons arrived with food from the Marcomanni. Heremigarius was with the convoy, and we could see that Ingamar wanted to confront him in front of his brother. Gaeser went to have a conversation with Hermeric and told me to restrain Ingamar from doing anything rash. When he returned, he explained that Hermeric was aware of what had happened and would deal with it himself. The food convoy was his attempt to make amends. We told Ingamar to let the matter lie. There was nothing to be gained from accusing Heremigarius in public.

When the Marcomanni had left us to return east, Gunderic explained that Hermeric was not yet ready to move his people south. The Marcomanni coveted the land of Germania Superior south of the

Rhine but would wait for the right time to cross. The Vandals and the Alans did not have the luxury of waiting for the right time. We all knew that the combined body of the remaining Asdings, the Alans and the soon-to-arrive Silings could not stay where we were in the middle of winter. We would starve to death. The Marcomanni supplies would only last for a day or two. We had to act soon.

As we were settling around our campfire that evening, a seasoned Vandal trooper approached us. We recognised him as one of Guntha's men. He sat with Gaeser for some time deep in conversation. Gaeser was hatching a plan but did not share it with me at that time.

The next day Guntha's man had left, and we rode across the plain with Gunderic and his remaining oathsworn. We took three wagonloads of food and requested an audience with Respendial. Gunderic apologised to Respendial for not coming sooner. The Asdings owed a great debt to the Alans for their timely arrival at the battle. We thanked them for their help and offered the food as a small token of our gratitude. Respendial was magnanimous in his victory and generous in his praise of the Vandals for their stubborn resistance. He was saddened to hear of the death of Godigsel. He offered for the Asdings to join with his people once they had crossed the river. Gunderic declined the offer, with thanks, but promised to work with the Alans in crossing the Rhine.

Respendial was as aware of the urgency of our situation as we were. He explained that the Alans had taken control of the unprotected bridge across the river Main. He said he had more than enough men to assault the castle protecting the main bridge across the Rhine. However, his losses attacking the bridge at Argentorate made him reluctant to repeat the experience. Gaeser spoke for the first time to dramatic effect.

"Lord King, I have a plan to cross the Rhine and, if it goes well, we will not lose any of our warriors."

Gaeser outlined his plans giving Respendial and Gunderic the timings they needed to support him. I was astonished at the sheer audacity of what he proposed to do. Gaeser intended to put the plan into action two days later.

The following day the Silings began to arrive. They camped to the east of the town and the battlefield. There were so many it would take five whole days for the entire tribe to cross the river Main. The Asding settlement in the abandoned town of Dieburg increasingly appeared as a small village between two vast cities with the Alans on one side and the Silings on the other. King Fredbal rode into town with his oathsworn around him. To our surprise, Sigibali and three young girls made up the party. The two kings went into a private conference.

Sigibali walked his horse towards us and Gaeser greeted him but immediately turned to the young girl beside him. He reached up to help Dagila dismount. The girl flung her arms around my brother and kissed him. Both the other girls moved directly to Ingamar and Kitan and greeted then in a similar fashion. I saw one or two hateful looks from young Vandal girls watching on and hoped it would not lead to violence. In no time their attention had switched to dismounted Siling oathsworn warriors and all was well. Sigibali had a wagon with barrels of mead and beer delivered to us. The celebration that evening was as merry as any I can remember.

It was late December and the weather had been freezing cold during the nights for some time, something we had not noticed when we had Franks camped all around us. Fortunately, there was no snow yet. We built up the fires as much as we could, hoping they would last through the night. Even so, many found it necessary to share their bodily warmth with another that night.

Gunderic explained in the morning that Fredbal had offered for the Asdings to join the Silings under Fredbal's leadership. Gunderic had declined. I think he would have found it difficult to serve under a younger man. Fredbal was hardly older than we were. Gunderic had told Fredbal that the

Asdings would remain a separate tribe despite the heavy losses we had suffered during the battle. Gaeser agreed and said that the Asdings should do as the Alans did and accept any into the tribe who would fight for us and adopt our ways. He was thinking of the Quadi, Alemanni and Pannonians who had fought bravely with us during the battle. We already thought of them as Asdings and many of them had taken up with Asding women since the battle in any case.

In the morning Gaeser assembled the mounted party he needed for his plan to cross the river. He took seventy Alemanni marines and one hundred and fifty Quadi soldiers, all instructed to wear a full Roman uniform if they had one. The companions would, of course, all come. I knew the part I was to play and wore my father's full regalia with the addition of my blue cloak. It fitted perfectly. We headed to Gernsheim, the river port on the Rhine, where we had previously seen the Rhine *classis* ships docked.

I knew the question Yannus would ask before he spoke.

"Master, some say that the Rhine froze that winter and that the Vandals and Alans rode across the river ice. Is it true?"

No, it is not true. Can you imagine how thick the river ice would have to have been to support thousands of heavy wagons going across it, not to mention hundreds of thousands of people and horses. If only it had been that simple. We crossed the Rhine by a great stratagem. Gaeseric would gain fame later for his clever strategy in taking Carthage from the Romans. His plan to cross the Rhine was a far cleverer stratagem in my opinion.

Chapter 26

Crossing the Rhine

At the river port of Gernsheim we found two *liburnae* from the Rhine *classis* tied up. Gaeser did not seem surprised. He took Ingamar and our Alemanni marines down to meet the ship captains and the Alemanni *classis ripenses*. The meeting seemed amicable, and our marines proceeded to man the ships. Gaeser explained that Guntha's trooper had brought news of the presence of Guntha's *ala* across the river opposite Gernsheim. Gaeser had sent him back with gold to bribe the Alemanni to let us use their ships both to cross the river and to sail up to Mogontiacum. We would leave seventy horses with them as surety for the return of the ships.

It took most of the day to ferry across all the Quadi soldiers and their horses as well as the companions and their barbs. Guntha's men were camped in a secluded spot close to the river with enough food to feed our small army. That evening the two groups swapped stories of their recent experiences. Guntha reported that after crossing the Rhine at Argentorate they had travelled north. Goar's Alans had travelled west and there had been no contact with them for several months. Guntha's *ala* had avoided the two Roman cities of

Novimagus and Borbetomagus along their route. The cities had substantial walls and Alemanni *foederati* garrisons. The Vandal troopers were able to shadow the movement of Respendial's Alans as they progressed north on the other side of the Rhine. They hadn't been sure where the Vandal convoys were but presumed that they must be further north than the Alans. The *ala* was a substantial force in an area that had no Roman forces at all save for the city garrisons. As such they were untroubled until they started to come across Rhine Frank villages on the outskirts of Mogontiacum. For the first time their attempts to buy food from the villages were rebuffed. Guntha decided to retire south opposite the river port. He sent a messenger across on the ferry with instructions to find Gaeseric.

The Quadi soldiers delighted in telling their account of the battle at Dieburg. They explained that the Rhine Frank warriors had reached the wagon barriers at the south of the town but had never crossed. The Quadi held the central position on the wall with the Vandal warriors on either side. The Vandal cavalry was embroiled in hand-to-hand fighting on both flanks of the Franks. They hailed Fredo as their hero and believed that, despite their heavy losses, they would have prevailed without the intervention of the Alans. As it was, the appearance of the Alans turned a close fight into a complete rout.

Tzason told Guntha's men of how he had found Respendial's Alans already moving to support the Vandals. Alan scouts had reported that the Franks had surrounded the Vandals in the abandoned town. Respendial sent out three separate forces. One to attack the southern Frank army, one to attack the northern Franks from the west and one to circle around the back of the northern Franks. Tzason was proud of the fact that the Alans had lost very few men in the battle.

Scarila was not to be outdone. He told of how he had found his people several weeks before, far to the north. They were moving at a snail's pace and Scarila failed to convince King Fredbal to send an advance party ahead to link up with the Asdings. It was only when Safrax found them and explained the urgency of the situation that Fredbal reacted. Moving on foot the Silings would have been unable to reach the battle in time to help. However, the king, his oathsworn and the Siling nobility were all mounted and they had raced back with Scarila and Safrax to join the battle.

Traso insisted on telling the story of how his brother had died and how he had had his horse killed from under him. He went on to tell of how Scarila and his friends had saved him by killing the Frank giant. It was fortunate that Ingamar was not with us because he was still consumed with anger over the actions of Heremigarius. Ingamar was across the river at the port. The next day he was to lead the two *liburnae*, crewed by our Alemanni marines, up-river to the Pons Ingeniosa.

I was now playing the part of a Roman general leading the advance guard of a relief army come north to protect Mongontiacum and the river crossing from the barbarian hoards. My armour, helmet and sword made that fiction entirely believable. Our barb horses and blue cloaks added a sense of status as did our "advance guard" of over 650 Vandal and Quadi auxiliaries. As we travelled up the Roman road, we sent regular scouts to the river to check on the progress of the two *liburnae*. The plan called for both parties to arrive at the same time.

The walled city was set back from the river by some distance, and we were able to bypass it and head directly for the bridge. The western side of the bridge had a small settlement clustered around it no doubt servicing the needs of the bridge garrison. Below the bridge a wooden jetty allowed river traffic to dock. A small fortress protected the bridge entrance. The fortress on the far side was formidable. We estimated the bridge garrison at full strength might number around a thousand men. Our column rode through the settlement huts and approached the smaller fortress. Rhine Frank guards blocked our path. The subterfuge began and I was the leading actor.

"I am General Marcus Flavius Eutychianus. General Saurus has sent me to relieve the city of

Mogontiacum and ensure that the barbarian hoards do not cross the Rhine. Go and fetch your commander. I will be taking over the defence of the bridge and the city."

We waited patiently for a reaction. All the troopers and soldiers were briefed to be alert and pick their targets should violence be needed. The Frank commander strode to the fortress wall. He looked suspicious.

"General, we have not been told of any relief force. We were not expecting you."

I replied in my best formal Latin adopting the superior tones of a Roman aristocrat.

"We sent messengers some time ago on a *laburnum* from Argentorate. We have assembled a force of 5,000 Goth auxiliaries, 2,000 Alemanni *foederati* with 4 *alae* of Gallic cavalry. They should be at Novimagus by now. We are the advance force. More troops will come by river. Once they are here, we will march out and confront the Alans camped across the river."

"You will need every one of your troops to defeat the Alans, General. There are over 10,000 of them over there. Plus any of the Vandals that survived the battle. I do not envy you your task. Until the relief force arrives, we will hold the bridge."

"No commander, you will not. You had your opportunity to defeat the invaders and you failed. General Saurus is displeased. You are to step down. My Quadi auxiliaries will garrison the bridge along with the Alemanni forces due to arrive. They will also garrison the city. Your orders are to evacuate your forces from the bridge fortresses and the city and join the garrison at Colonia."

The commander looked uncertain as to how to process the information he was hearing. It was at that point that the two *liburnae* arrived at the jetty below. Ingamar came jogging up the steps with an honour guard of Alemanni marines, stamping to attention in front of me.

Ingamar spoke the words Gaeser had prepared for him.

"General Eutychianus. General Saurus sends his regards. The relief forces are now at Borbetomagus. He wishes you to approach the Alans under truce and attempt to recruit them to the Gallic army. The Britannia legions have revolted and raised one of their own to the purple. General Saurus believes they are about to invade Gaul. The army cannot be delayed here. We must move west as soon as possible to confront them. Ideally with a few thousand newly recruited Alan auxiliaries. The Alans will be granted land in Gaul in return for their service. There is no time to lose"

I barked my response at the commander.

"You heard the man, commander. Get your men off the bridge now. Open the gates. I wish to go across and talk to the Alans. If I find you here when

I return, I will have your head. Commander Fredo you have command of the bridge. Commander Guntha, form an escort. Let's go and talk to the barbarians. Find a peace symbol so they don't attack us."

And it worked. The greatest deception I was ever a part of. The Franks left the bridge. There were, in fact, only 400 of them. They went to the city. Within an hour the garrison was leaving on the road north to Colonia.

I so enjoyed my role that I was tempted to continue with it as we rode across the bridge and out of the fortress gates. Gunderic and Respendial rode forward to meet us. Gunderic was enjoying the spectacle and called out.

"General Scuta, is it not. What news from the bridge?"

"The bridge is ours. We may cross whenever we want."

Respendial was delighted.

"Well done boys. This has saved many lives. I think the Asdings should have the honour of crossing first."

Gaeser advised us to wait until the morning before crossing. He explained.

"The gates of the city are still closed to us now, but the Rhine Frank garrison is leaving. When the civilian population realises their situation they are likely to panic. We should hold back and let them flee out of the gates on the far side. In the morning

I predict that every gate on the far side will be open. We can simply ride around the city and enter. We can easily catch the refugees on the road if we wish to."

The two kings agreed and returned to their respective encampments for the night. The companions and Guntha's *ala* joined Fredo and the Quadi in the bridge castle where we celebrated our success and started planning for the next day. At first light on the first day of the year 407, Gunderic rode through the castle and across the bridge with his oathsworn while Respendial and his senior warband leaders followed just behind. Gaeser led the companions after them. As he had anticipated, the richer citizens had evacuated the city taking all the portable wealth they could manage. They would carry the message to the rest of the Roman world. The Vandals and Alans had crossed the Rhine.

The end.

✠ ✠ ✠

Follow the adventures of Gaeseric, Scuta and the companions as the Vandals and Alans rampage through Gaul in the next book in The Vandals series:

THE VANDALS
Book 2 – Rampage through Gaul.

Printed in Great Britain
by Amazon